# The Neuropsychology of Reading Disorders:

## Diagnosis and Intervention workbook

Steven G. Feifer, Ed.S., NCSP    Philip A. De Fina, Ph.D., ABPdN

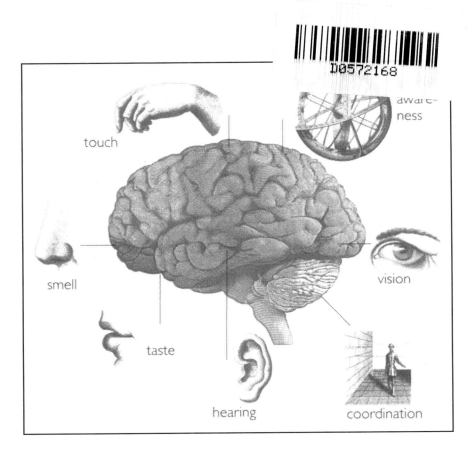

touch

awareness

smell

vision

taste

hearing

coordination

Foreword by Elkhonon Goldberg, Ph.D.

# ACKNOWLEDGMENTS

Our heartfelt thanks and appreciation to all who encouraged and assisted in this worthy endeavor. In particular, George McCloskey for reviewing the initial manuscript and offering salient comments while still leaving us optimistic enough to see the project through. A very special thanks to our editorial consultant, Amy Eutsey, who somehow found the time and energy to work despite two new additions to the family, and to the *Wizard of Word,* Martha Specht, whose secretarial and computer skills were critical in this project. Also, a special feeling of gratitude to the many clinicians who made contributions to this workbook, especially the professors in the post-graduate neuropsychology specialty program at the Fielding Institute. Lastly, much appreciation to Frederick County Public School's Dyslexia Program for their input and assistance on the intervention section. As always, a loving acknowledgment to Darci and Lisa for putting up with two very obsessive-compulsive brains.

The Neuropsychology of Reading Disorders: Diagnosis and Intervention Workbook by Steven G. Feifer and Philip A. De Fina; foreword by Elkhonon Goldberg

Published by School Neuropsych Press, LLC
PO Box 413
Middletown, MD  21769
Snpress@frederickmd.com

Cover photograph adapted from *Mapping the Mind,* by R. Carter, p. 115, University of California Press, Copyright 1998 by Weidenfeld & Nicholson. Reprinted with permission. Cover designed by Octavo Designs in Frederick, Maryland.

ISBN # 0-9703337-0-6

Printed in the United States of America

# DEDICATION

*To Brendan and Madison, whose loving spirit will always provide the inspiration and drive behind all future endeavors.* —SGF

*To Alexandra, my loving daughter whose creativity and high energy level will always be a driving force in my life.* —PAD

# FOREWORD

I am delighted that the *Neuropsychology of Reading Disorders: Diagnosis and Intervention Workbook* is being prepared. The interface of neuropsychological and educational issues is among the most pertinent and exciting frontiers of clinical research and practice. This expertly written workbook, containing a rich collection of illustrative clinical cases, will provide a unique and invaluable didactic source for the students of neuropsychology and school psychology. It will help advance this new and exciting field of neuropsychological applications in the educational community.

Elkhonon Goldberg, Ph.D., ABPP/ABCN
Clinical Professor of Neurology
NYU School of Medicine

# INTRODUCTION

This workbook was not intended to be a comprehensive textbook for the neuropsychology of reading disorders, but rather to serve as a practical guide for clinicians and educators. The impetus behind this manuscript was to assist psychologists and educators in appreciating and understanding the complexities of developmental dyslexia within the context of a brain-based education model. It was the intention of the authors to portray these disorders from the perspective of the cognitive neuropsychologist. Brain-behavioral paradigms have been virtually ignored in traditional psychological and educational assessments resulting in reports and interventions that have limited value for children. It is imperative that diagnostic tools be utilized and interpreted with an appropriate level of sophistication that will assist in facilitating meaningful intervention strategies. This workbook will enable clinicians and educators to realize the relevance of integrating brain-behavioral models of assessment with traditional pedagological interventions. It is replete with practical information that should enhance the diagnostic prowess of the clinician, assist in crafting an appropriate IEP for a child, and hopefully aid in the educational remediation of dyslexia.

—The Authors

# table of contents

# overview

# Chapter I

Reading and literacy are relatively new phenomena, encompassing approximately the last 5000 to 6000 years of human history. The influence of literacy goes beyond the scope of shaping our culture and fueling the technological advances of human civilization. To some, literacy may be at the forefront of understanding the cerebral organization and functional adaptability of the human brain. Clearly, the ability to synthesize and analyze visual codes into meaningful thinking and communication has been the hallmark of higher education, and is the mainstay for success in school. While literacy estimates have ranged from 75 to 90 percent in the United States, approximately one-third of the world's population remains illiterate (Roselli, 1993). Exposure to linguistically rich environments coupled with high quality education has factored heavily into a child's ability to read. However, the biological mechanisms which allow reading to develop in an unfettered fashion appears to be at the root for most reading disorders. Unfortunately, some in the American education system have been reluctant to accept the notion of a biological basis to reading disorders. Frivolous explanations such as a distracting home environment, "laziness", or a host of social factors have been endorsed to justify why students have difficulty with reading and derive limited school success. Notwithstanding, many special education classes in our schools are *curricular-driven,* which is nothing more than slower paced instruction, as opposed to a specially designed strategic intervention plan targeted to enhance the student's unique learning ability.

Additionally, there is a growing educational *fad* in which norm-referenced testing is not being utilized. Instead, it is being replaced by a *curriculum based* assessment model, which is targeted at changing the educational environment without a proper

understanding of the child's neurocognitive strengths and weaknesses. This is extremely problematic, in that it attempts to *fix* the curriculum rather than assist the child in developing effective compensatory strategies for learning. Furthermore, delaying the process of early comprehensive neuropsychological and educational assessments may result in a student's inability to optimally benefit from subsequent, later special education procedures. This is due to reduced neural plasticity within an older child's brain, creating a situation in which the *window of opportunity* for learning critical elements of the reading process becomes substantially reduced and eventually lost. For instance, there is a growing body of research stemming from the neuropsychological literature suggesting that children who have not mastered the phonemic code to reading by age 10 may never acquire this skill (Rourke & Del Dotto, 1994). Consequently, older neurocognitively *impaired* children, who may have been denied early intervention services due to limitations in diagnostic procedures, now present with an unfortunate dilemma in that they are somewhat impervious to change. Special education now becomes a last resort measure analogous to a palliative treatment regimen, rather than one that will have substantial long-term effectiveness. In other words, it can be likened to a person who does not receive appropriate medical intervention during the early stages of a disease, thus rendering them unlikely to benefit from potentially curative medicine given at a later date.

The most widely accepted paradigm for diagnosing reading disabilities relied heavily upon aptitude/achievement discrepancies. Hence, the average age in which a child is classified as reading disabled is 9 years old, or 3rd grade, since this is when discrepancies become most prevalent (Shaywitz, 1998). Since this leaves such a short remaining window of opportunity, perhaps this is why 74% of children classified as learning disabled in 3rd grade remain so through 9th grade (Lyon, 1996). Therefore, appropriate intervention needs to commence much earlier for children, when the brain is at a critical juncture for phoneme classification and language processing. In sum, psychologists need to embark on a new and more effective paradigm for understanding, remediating, and improving reading disorders in children. The primary objectives of this workbook will be to:

1) Discuss the fallacies of relying solely upon an aptitude/achievement discrepancy model to evaluate reading disorders in young children.

2) Link brain functions to the reading process and introduce a *brain-based* educational model to effectively identify and classify subtypes of reading disorders.

3)     Discuss the various subtypes of reading disabilities from a neurobehavioral point of view, and tie in appropriate educational strategies for each subtype.

The term developmental dyslexia refers to an inability to acquire functional reading skills despite the presence of normal intelligence <u>and</u> exposure to adequate educational opportunities. Developmental dyslexia represents the most common type of learning disability, affecting an estimated 5 to 10 percent of school-age population, and assumes a neurological base (Shaywitz, 1998). Efforts to understand the neurobiological mechanisms related to dyslexia have focused on those neural systems serving language, primarily in the perisylvian association cortex in the left hemisphere (Schultz, et al., 1994). Due to the strong familial trends, dyslexia is believed to be a genetically based disorder that is expressed in a heterogeneous manner, with probably as many unique forms as there are individuals diagnosed with it. However, for classification purposes, there have been generalized subtypes that have emerged.

Reading disorders have been classified under three distinct rubrics: Approximately two-thirds of children with a reading disorder are ***dysphonetic*** readers, and have difficulty processing information through auditory channels. This is a basic phonological processing disorder affecting reading, spelling and written language. In essence, these children have poor decoding skills, and the essential features of sound/symbol associations have not been mastered. Consequently, dysphonetic readers over-rely on their sight vocabulary to generate *visual images* of words and have extreme difficulty reading nonwords. Once again, some research has suggested that children who have not mastered the phonetic code to reading by age 10 will never acquire this skill (Rourke & Del Dotto, 1994).

***Surface dyslexia*** represents approximately 14 percent of reading disabilities, and is characterized by difficulty visualizing words in a fashion where reading becomes automatic. Consequently, these children read at a slower pace, tend to over-rely on sound/symbol associations, and make errors on frequently encountered words. In other words, these types of readers tend to break every word down in a phonetic manner, and reading never becomes an automatic, fluid type of process. While phonological processing is critical to early reading development, skilled readers rely heavily on the ability to automatically recognize words based upon the contour of shapes. Some have referred to this subtype as having a nonverbal learning disability, as social skills deficits are often seen as well. Specific neuropsychological traits of this group often include deficits in visual/spatial analysis and synthesis.

The third type is the most severe form known as **mixed dyslexia,** and involves reading, spelling, and written language disorders characteristic of both dysphonetic and visual-spatial subtypes. These children often become severely impaired learners, as there is no usable key to decipher the reading and spelling code. Most educators agree that skilled readers rely on an interactive system that taps <u>both</u> phonological and visual memory stores simultaneously. Research has suggested that the inability to transfer information between both hemispheres may be at the core of phonological (difficulty accessing left hemisphere) and visual (difficulty accessing right hemisphere) dyslexia (Bakker, 1992). From a brain-behavioral perspective, this can be attributed to deficits in the major bands of interconnective tissue between the hemispheres, namely, the *corpus callosum.*

Other low incidence subtypes of dyslexia worthy of discussion are neurological variations such as **dejerine syndrome,** which is dyslexia in the absence of a specific writing disorder, **deep dyslexia,** which is an impairment in reading comprehension, and **hyperlexia,** a condition characterized by the uncanny ability to recognize words despite severe cognitive limitations in comprehension. All of these reading variations lend credence that distinct neural pathways subserve different aspects of this complex task called reading. A brief discussion of this neural circuitry will shed light on the subtle nuances of reading disabilities, and how such unusual conditions are possible. In addition, having a basic understanding of brain/behavior relationships should facilitate appropriate remediation strategies.

Lastly, there will be a discussion on specific neuropsychological tests used to tease out unique features of reading. For instance, early developmental signs such as rapid naming tasks, speed of retrieval of over-learned verbal labels (colors, letters, numbers, etc.), and accuracy of nonword reading can be used as early predictors of reading difficulty. Much emphasis will be placed on using a **process oriented** approach, which analyzes error patterns, as opposed to relying solely on a quantitative, or **level of performance** approach, when evaluating children. Finally, specific remediation and compensation strategies will be discussed, with both the subtype of reading disability and developmental stage of reading dictating the intervention.

---

*****Alexia,** an acquired form of reading disability attributed to the onset of neurological disease or trauma, will not be addressed in this workbook.

# TEN PITFALLS OF DISCREPANCY MODEL

# Chapter 2

*"science is more than a body of knowledge and accumulated facts, for it represents a way of thinking."*
*— carl sagan, cosmos.*

Since its inception in 1975, perhaps no other documentation or single piece of legislation has profoundly impacted the nature of psychological evaluations more than Public Law 94-142, the Education for All Handicapped Children Act. While ensuring that all children have a right to a free and appropriate public education, the law also established safeguards for the evaluation and placement of children in special education programs. Specifically, the law stipulated that state and local education agencies ensure that tests are administered by trained professionals, in the child's native language, and that no single procedure be used as the sole criterion for determining an appropriate educational program. In addition, testing and evaluation materials must be selected and administered so as not to be racially or culturally discriminatory, and all evaluations need to be completed by a multi-disciplinary team including a specialist with knowledge in the suspected area of disability. Overall, the law represents an attempt by the federal government to ensure that handicapped children receive a meaningful, fair, and nondiscriminatory education.

While the efforts have been noble, the results of PL 94-142 have been somewhat controversial as ambiguous definitions, procedural loopholes, and inconsistent interpretations have been fodder for aggressive lawyers and dismayed parents. Included

in the regulations for the implementation of PL 94-142 lies specific criteria for the definition and classification of each handicapping condition. With respect to a specific learning disability, the following definition is postulated:

*"Specific learning disability means a disorder in one or more of the basic psychological processes involved in understanding or in using language, spoken or written, which may manifest itself in an imperfect ability to listen, think, speak, read, write, spell, or perform mathematical calculations. The term includes such conditions as perceptual handicaps, brain injury, minimal brain dysfunction, dyslexia, and developmental aphasia. The term does not include children who have learning problems which are primarily the result of visual, hearing or motor handicaps, of mental retardation, of emotional disturbance, or of environmental, cultural, or economic disadvantage (Sattler, p. 598)."*

Notwithstanding, Public Law 94-142 also dictated that a designation of specific learning disability should be applied only to children who have a severe discrepancy between achievement and intellectual ability in one or more receptive skills, such as written expression, listening and reading, comprehension, and/or mathematics. The discrepancy cannot be the result of sensory handicaps, mental retardation, emotional disturbance, or environmental, cultural, or economic disadvantage. Hence, the official genesis of the **discrepancy model** became entrenched and dominated the field of school psychology by dictating special education placement decisions for decades to come. Despite amendments to the law in 1986 (Public Law 99-457), and most recently IDEA in 1997, no guidelines were established to indicate how a severe discrepancy should be determined. Furthermore, the law insinuated that the presence of a discrepancy automatically lead to a handicapping condition without addressing possible reasons for the disparity in scores. Consequently, most school districts relied on a *level of performance* approach to identifying handicapping conditions in children, concentrating merely on overall test score performances while ignoring important neuropsychological and perceptual functions which so richly portray each student's learning needs. The result has lead to *administrative* assessments for classification purposes and provided little information about a student's unique learning needs. Furthermore, little information can be garnered for an effective IEP relying on the *level of performance* model of assessing children. Hence, a rift emerged in psychology between the bureaucratic assessments stipulated by the law versus scientific assessments based upon brain/behavior relationships. There are multiple pitfalls for relying upon an aptitude/achievement based model for diagnosing learning disabilities in children. Notwithstanding, here are just 10 reasons why such a model should be disregarded:

## 1. There is no universal agreement on what the discrepancy should be.

The term *dyslexia* has been plagued by definition confusion and inconsistency since its inception (Lyon, 1996). Consequently, systems for delivery of special education services tend to vary from state to state as educators grapple with the true meaning of this term. At least four means are available for evaluating a discrepancy between ability and achievement. These involve deviation from grade or age level, expectancy formulas, regression equations, and standard score comparisons. For example, in the state of Maryland, local systems are free to adopt any method to operationally define a learning disability, with most districts relying on a 1.5 standard deviation rule of thumb to determine a discrepancy. Furthermore, age equivalents are generally used as the basis for the discrepancy. However, some neighboring school districts in the state of West Virginia rely on regression equations based upon age and grade norms to determine a learning disability, while some southern districts in the state of Virginia use a strict *cut point* system between standard scores to determine a discrepancy. In other words, depending on which side of the Potomac River a student resides can determine whether a child receives special education services.

## 2. It remains unclear as to which IQ score should be used to establish a discrepancy.

The unwritten rule of thumb for many psychologists postulates that when a significant verbal/performance discrepancy exists, use the higher of the two scores to indicate a student's cognitive potential. For instance, if a student had a Verbal IQ of 90, a Performance IQ of 105 (thus a significant difference), and a Full Scale IQ of 97, the higher of the scores or Performance IQ score (105) would be assumed to best estimate cognitive functioning. However, if this same student had a Verbal IQ of 90, a Performance IQ of 104 (not significant), and a Full Scale IQ of 96, the Full Scale score (96) would be used as the best estimate of cognitive functioning. A difference of one point on the Performance scale would result in a nine-point difference (105 vs. 96) in scores. The difference of nine points may not sound like much, but when school systems use strict cut points to measure discrepancies, it can determine whether or not a child receives special education services. This philosophy assumes intelligence is a unitary construct that can be quantitatively defined by a single score, as opposed to a unique array of processing attributes that define a student's specific learning style. Furthermore, according to Kaufman (1994), approximately one in four children displays a statistically significant discrepancy (15 points at .01 level) between their verbal and performance subtests. Therefore, significant discrepancies are fairly common in the normal population and should not be used to automatically detect cognitive abnormalities.

### 3. A discrepancy model of reading disabilities precludes early identification.

According to Rourke & Del Dotto (1994), children who have not developed phonological awareness by age 9 or 10 probably have lost the capacity to do so. As will be discussed in the next section, the brain is the ultimate reductionistic organ. In other words, cells which are responsible for processing sounds in a symbolic fashion will decline when not used and eventually die out (pruning) or find another functional means to gravitate towards (Kotulak, 1997). Therefore, early identification is crucial toward the remediation of dyslexia due to the functional plasticity of many neural pathways. Since the average age which children are classified as reading disabled is 9 years old or 3rd grade, this is almost too late for effective interventions to take place. Perhaps this is why 74% of children who are classified as reading disabled in 3rd grade remain so through 9th grade (Lyon, 1996). Furthermore, behavior difficulties and poor academic motivation often result following years of mounting academic frustration.

### 4. Intelligence is more a predictor of school success, and not necessarily a predictor of successful reading.

According to Lyon (1996), a meta-analysis of the research in reading suggests that the best predictor of future reading success for kindergarten and first grade students is phoneme recognition. Furthermore, Denkla (1976) found that color-naming speed tended to differentiate dyslexic readers from other children as well. Therefore, the best indicators of future reading success among young children stems from phonological awareness coupled with rapid and automatic recognition of letters. Unfortunately, most school psychologists continue to rely solely on IQ tests as an abstract correlate for a student's "potential" for successful reading. Consequently, many students are not identified as being "at risk" for reading difficulty at younger ages, when interventions have a much greater opportunity to elicit success. Recent longitudinal studies by Wolf (1999) continue to validate naming speed as a viable and powerful predictor of kindergarten children at risk for reading difficulty. In fact, naming speed is a more effective predictor of children with reading difficulty than both IQ and phonological awareness in more orthographically regular languages such as German, Dutch, Finnish, and French. Interestingly, some students have a condition known as hyperlexia, which is the uncanny ability to decode words *despite significant cognitive deficiencies*. Therefore, IQ tests should not be used as the sole predictor of future reading skills in children as the relationship between IQ and reading does not appear to be linear.

**5. There is no evidence to suggest that poor readers on the lower end of the reading distribution differ from individuals classified as dyslexic.**

According to research published by Siegal (1992), poor readers or garden variety readers do not differ from dyslexics on reading, spelling, memory, or language measures. The only difference between the two groups once IQ was accounted for was that the dyslexic group was better at math and most visual spatial types of tasks. Therefore, there is no real difference between poor readers and children classified as dyslexics in that both groups have significant deficits in phonological processing, verbal memory, and syntactical awareness. This finding dilutes the popular argument that a student must have at least average intelligence to be classified as reading disabled, since both average and below average students generally have the same pitfalls with respect to reading. Hence, the relationship between reading and IQ is most likely bidirectional, in that intelligence test scores will fall over time with children who are not reading (Siegal, 1989). Unfortunately, many students of low average intelligence have *fallen between the cracks* and been denied services or simply have been labeled as being *slow learners* working up to their ability. The research that students with higher IQ's will be able to use better compensatory strategies remains mixed.

**6. It is illogical to utilize just one method to calculate a reading disability when research from the neuropsychological literature has documented numerous subtypes of reading disabilities.**

One of the most common fallacies and false assumptions about dyslexia and other learning disabilities is that they represent a homogeneous population. Each student represents a unique challenge as educators grapple with the most effective teaching methodology to satisfy the composite learning needs of a child. The next section will point out various types of reading disabilities, including *dysphonetic dyslexia, surface dyslexia, mixed dyslexia,* and *deep dyslexia.* Each subtype of dyslexia represents a breakdown along the brain's neural pathway with respect to reading. Relying on an aptitude/achievement model for diagnosing learning disabilities yields little information with respect to subtyping specific reading disorders as well as eliciting appropriate intervention strategies. In other words, the conceptual paradigm of treating learning disabilities must reflect the subtle nuances of each learner based upon the integrity of basic brain-behavior relationships with respect to academic functioning.

**7. Discrepancy models are not developmentally sensitive toward different stages of reading at different age groups.**

Most elementary students have difficulty with phonological awareness and word recognition skills, whereas secondary students often struggle with reading speed, fluency, and comprehension. These specific subcomponents of reading are often overlooked because psychologists tend to focus on numeric discrepancies to qualify students for special education classes. In fact, there is no specific law or regulation that differentiates the numeric value of a discrepancy between a first-grader versus a ninth-grader. In other words, most school districts employ a rigid point structure or cut-off score to be applied to all learners at all ages regardless of developmental appropriateness. Consequently, research has shown that relying on a discrepancy model would identify just 2% of all first graders since these tests are not sensitive for this age group. Conversely, nearly 25% of ninth-graders would have a significant discrepancy using this same methodology for identification of a learning disability (Kolb & Whishaw, 1996). Therefore, this approach tends to *under-identify* young children and *over-identify* older students, leading to inconsistent educational decisions and precluding early identification.

**8. A discrepancy model promotes a wait and fail policy forcing interventions to come after the fact.**

Most school districts believe a child must be reading at least two grade levels below to be considered reading disabled. Therefore, the child has probably undergone years of academic failure, experienced problems of low self esteem, and probably developed some behavior difficulties before being identified. A discrepancy model is a reactive means to identify children, and certainly not a proactive method as important neurolinguistic variables are often overlooked. Furthermore, interventions become all the more difficult to employ as most children have already developed a negative attitude and poor academic motivation as a means for coping with their limited school success.

**9. Discrepancy formulas often do not detect subtle neurological variations such as organization and attention problems, poor memory and retrieval skills, and dyspraxias and dysphasias. In other words, they are far too simplistic.**

Once again, relying solely upon a level of performance approach and not examining specific psychological processes and patterns of learning leads to *administrative assessments*. In other words, students are assessed for the purpose of rubber stamping a label on them, boxing them into a particular category, and little information is given to both explain and remediate specific cognitive deficits that impact on learning.

## 10. Discrepancy formulas are often adjusted to regulate funding for special education.

It costs virtually three times more money to educate a student in special education than a student in regular education. Consequently, most local jurisdictions have a spending cap determined by the state, usually allocating reimbursement for up to 16-18 percent of enrolled students in need of special education services. In other words, funding dictates the number of students a given school district can identify as being handicapped. Though not implicitly stated, school districts often readjust their identification criteria based upon the cap in order to continue to receive state and federal funds. Therefore, discrepancy models serve as a very efficient methodological framework to operate under since numbers can easily be adjusted forward or backward. Hence, tinkering with a regression equation, dictating only a particular psychometric instrument be used (i.e. Woodcock-Johnson), or adopting a new standard deviation can be employed to increase or decrease the percentage of students in need of services. Once again, the bureaucracy side of psychology instead of the scientific side of psychology appears at the forefront of today's educational climate.

# Hemispheric specialization & cerebral Dominance

# Chapter 3

Most DNA evidence suggests that the human brain has been evolving for approximately five million years. It remains unfathomable that a cluster of nerve cells can dictate our thoughts, moods, memories, and experiences not to mention our own self-consciousness. However, within the electromagnetic fields created by brain chemicals, known collectively as *neurotransmitters,* it does just that. There is no doubt that the human brain cell marked a critical leap in evolution by its ability to form flexible connections with other cells and eventually send and receive electrochemical messages. The human brain has approximately 100 billion neurons and glial or support cells. To add perspective, a piece of your brain about the size of a grain of sand would contain one hundred thousand neurons, two million axons, and one billion synapses talking to each other (Ramachandran, 1998). In layman's terms, the human brain is about as big as a coconut, the shape of a walnut, the color of uncooked liver, and the consistency of chilled butter (Carter, 1998). However, it is the newest addition to our brains, the neocortex, which largely separates humans from other species in that we have four times more thickness than any other primate (Calvin & Ojemann, 1994). Remarkably, the language centers of our brains have evolved to allow for the rapid and automatic recognition of symbols to convey meaningful thought and spur abstract ideas. Namely, human beings have the amazing capacity to speak, read, and write.

The term **neuropsychology** is a hybrid utilizing both a medical and psychological model of human functioning that examines brain-behavioral relationships. The underlying assumption is that the brain is the seat of all behavior; therefore, knowledge of cerebral organization should be the key to unlocking the mystery behind most cognitive tasks. Perhaps the central issue in neuropsychology over the past 100 years has been the question of how psychological functions are represented in our brains. An analysis of the specific brain regions associated with dyslexia have come from electroencephalography (EEG) measures, magnetic resonance imaging (MRI) studies, regional cerebral blood flow profiles (rCBF), positron emission tomography (PET) studies, and postmortem examinations. Multi-model imaging is becoming increasingly popular, combining two or more of these techniques to give a more complete picture (Carter, 1998). It seems apparent that discerning the qualities of skilled versus unskilled readers requires an understanding of the specific neurocognitive elements involved in reading, and their corresponding brain-behavioral relationships.

The human brain can be divided by its structure into two physical units, or hemispheres. Each hemisphere is virtually identical in structure to the other, with the exception of the pineal gland that sits in the center base of our brain. Nevertheless, both hemispheres are not symmetrical in their physical structure as subtle differences exist. For instance, the right hemisphere extends a bit further forward than the left hemisphere, and the left temporal lobe is somewhat larger than the right temporal lobe (Kolb & Whishaw, 1996). Furthermore, the right hemisphere tends to be slightly larger and heavier than the left hemisphere, though there is more gray matter in the left hemisphere. While subtle structural variations distinguish each hemisphere, the functional differences of each side of the brain are more pronounced. A simplified study of the contributions of our brain's hemispheres to intellectual functions is as follows (Storfer, 1990):

## TABLE 3-1

### A SIMPLIFIED SUMMARY OF THE CONTRIBUTIONS OF OUR BRAIN'S HEMISPHERES TO INTELLECTUAL FUNCTION

(From *Intelligence and Giftedness: The Contribution of Heredity and Early Environment,* by M.D. Storfer, 1990, p. 340, San Francisco: Jossey-Bass. Copyright 1990 by Jossey-Bass. Reprinted with permission.)

| Dimension | Right Hemisphere | Left Hemisphere |
|---|---|---|
| Mode of Analysis | Excels at visualizing a whole (forming an entire picture out of its component parts) | Excels in performing an analytical, serial, or segmental breakdown of a whole into its component parts |
| Integration of Inputs | Better at integrating inputs from several modalities (for example, vision and hearing); better at "parallel processing" | Better at unimodal processing (that is, processing stimuli from one sensory mode); better at serial (sequential) processing |
| Novelty-Practice | More adept at coping with novel stimuli, particularly if no familiar contextual mechanisms are readily discernible | Contains a store of information contexts within which to analyze a task |
| Judgmental Mode | Better at purely physical judgements (structural similarities) | Better at categorical judgments (for example, conceptual or functional similarities) |
| Emotional | Recognizes emotional content; contains most of our emotional reactivity; contains mostly pessimistic emotions | Cannot recognize the emotional content of stories, despite understanding the literal meaning; contains many of our optimistic feelings |
| Facial Recognition | Predominates due to its visuo-spatial and emotional processing superiorities | Involved in very difficult or categorical judgments or recognizing very familiar faces |
| Attention | Better at sustained attention and at paying attention to environmental stimuli; engaged by high arousal | Better at focused attention to analytical processes than to surroundings; better at "quiet concentration" |
| Arithmetic | Responsible for initial arrangement and alignment of columns and for "global conceptualizations" of methodology | Calculation involves primarily the left hemisphere |
| Music | Better at perceiving pitch, timbre (melodic contour), and unfamiliar melodies; used more by untrained listeners | Better at sequential, time-dependent aspects of music comprehension and at recognizing familiar melodies; used more by trained musicians |
| Verbal Skills (nonspeech) | Processes considerable comprehensive abilities; organizes information at the paragraph level; understands the metaphorical meaning and the emotional content of words | Undertakes most aspects of language comprehension; understands the literal meaning of words |
| Speech | Can utter expletives (curses) and possibly "sing" words | Performs virtually all facets of language expression (in almost all people) |

The term ***cerebral dominance*** has become quite fashionable in the world of popular psychology to describe superficial personality characteristics of individuals. For instance, many creative and artful minded souls have been deemed *right-brain* thinkers, while dutiful, structured, and somewhat rigid individuals have been coined *left-brain* thinkers. In reality, these terms are used more as metaphors to provide behavioral descriptions as opposed to specific road maps that reveal the preferred anatomical locations of our temperamental make-up. In neuropsychology, the term ***cerebral dominance*** generally refers to the lateralization of language functions, as nearly 99 percent of right-handers and 67 percent of left-handers have virtually all language functions housed in the left hemisphere (Kolb & Whishaw, 1996). Interestingly, language functions tend to be more lateralized in males than females (Shaywitz, 1996). In other words, there appears to be gender differences in brain organization for cognitive functions. For instance, in males, most reading centers are located primarily in the left hemisphere, leaving little "back up" if damage occurs to this area. However, in females, reading centers seemed to be housed in both hemispheres, leaving the intact hemisphere to assume language functions when damage to one hemisphere occurs (Goldberg & Costa, 1981). Perhaps this is why male stroke patients often lose speech, whereas female stroke patients are able to retain language skills. With respect to the developing brain of a child, it seems plausible that the preponderance of boys in special education might be due in part to the lateralization of language centers in the male brain, leaving few alternative avenues to process linguistic information when there is damage to this region.

# Higher cortical functions

# Chapter 4

Like an archeologist sifting through ruins to find a lost civilization or a geologist chiseling beneath the earth's crust to peek at earlier rock formations, modern neuroscientists have accepted the notion that the human brain has also evolved in a series of layers. Therefore, to comprehend the complexities of higher cortical functions such as reading and written language, an analysis of more primitive lower cortical functions should provide the basis for understanding the evolution of reading. According to MacLean (1973), the triune brain hypothesis states that we actually have three brains, each anatomically layered above the more primitive one, yet clearly set apart by leaps in evolution. Our primitive ***reptilian brain*** is composed of the brain stem, cerebellum, and hypothalamus. In addition to providing basic life support functions and general levels of arousal, the reptilian brain controls stereotyped behaviors that enable us to deal reflexively with the external environment. For instance, opening our eyes wide with surprise, showing our teeth when angered, withdrawing with fear, and our body language in courtship behavior are automatic reflexes evolving over millions of years. The major goal of our reptilian brain is survival of the species, with norepinephrine being a key neurotransmitter in this region.

The next critical juncture in brain evolution is the emotional brain, which is comprised mainly of the limbic system. The limbic system regulates emotional states by interfacing with basic survival drives of lower brain regions (reptilian brain), and higher cortical functions in the cerebral cortex. In other words, this region has two-way connections with both the cerebral cortex, lying above, and with lower brain centers.

Major structural components of the limbic system include the **hippocampus,** which is responsible for laying down new memories, and the **amygdala,** which designates an emotional charge to incoming stimuli and primarily is responsible for emotional arousal. Also included is the **accumbens nucleus,** which is involved in self-reinforcing types of behavior and serves as the brain reward or pleasure center. A major neurotransmitter that sets the emotional tone for much of our behavior is serotonin, though dopamine plays a vital role in both the brain reward centers as well as modulating the **basal ganglia,** a vital component for automatic motor movements.

Approximately one and a half million years ago, the brain underwent an explosive enlargement, pushing the bones of the skull outward, creating the high, flat forehead which distinguishes us from our primates (Carter, 1998). The frontal lobes of the brain expanded by about 40 percent to create large areas of new gray matter, the **neocortex.** The neocortex is the newest addition to our brain and though made up of just six layers of nerve cells, serves to regulate our conscious lives by allowing us to integrate and modulate our perceptions into higher levels of thought. Comprised of primarily gray matter, this brain region is the realm of intuition, abstract thought, planning and reflecting, and critical analysis. It is here that we have ideas and inspirations, here that we speak, read and write, calculate mathematics, and compose music. This region is served by neurotransmitters such as dopamine, a factor in attention and concentration as well as physical motivation; as well as GABA, a neurotransmitter which serves as a **STOP** switch, thereby inhibiting cells from firing (Kotulak, 1997); and serotonin. Thus, it is the cerebral cortex that allows us to delay gratifying our emotional impulses and embark on a more mature and cognitively satisfying existence. With respect to reading, the cerebral cortex is primarily responsible for the ability to comprehend a symbolic code into linguistically rich and meaningful thoughts that allow us to communicate our insights and feelings like no other species on the planet.

The cerebral cortex can be divided into four primary lobes, each with a specific function to carry out the division of labor which fuels our conscious lives. The **occipital lobe** forms the posterior pole of the brain and processes visual input. There are over 30 distinct visual areas in the brain, each specialized in either color, form, or motion (Ramachandran, 1998). However, with respect to vision, there appears to be two major pathways, the more primitive *how* pathway, and the newer *what* pathway. The newer *what* pathway is a visual neural circuit whereby incoming visual stimuli travels from the lateral geniculate nucleus of the thalamus to the occipital lobes for higher level processing. The information is then sent to either the temporal lobes for recognition of an object, as well as to the parietal lobes to tell where an object is in space. The cortical-cortical

pathways subserve functions for object discrimination (i.e. shapes of letters, contours of words, etc.). This is the ventral occipitotemporal pathway for object discrimination. The neural mechanisms go from striate to prestriate to inferotemporal cortex. There is also a dorsal pathway that assists in discerning spatial orientation and spatial relationships that are necessary for reading fluency. The pathway goes from the striate cortex to the prestriate region and finally to the posterior parietal cortex. The cortical to subcortical circuitry subserves the processes of object identification, object localization, and focal vision. These functions are modulated within the retinogeniculostriate pathways.

## fIGURE 4-I

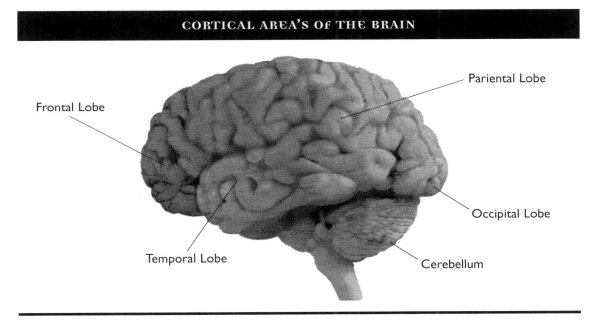

CORTICAL AREA'S OF THE BRAIN

Frontal Lobe

Pariental Lobe

Temporal Lobe

Occipital Lobe

Cerebellum

Conversely, the older *how* pathway operates on an unconscious level as visual information travels not to the occipital lobes, but rather down to the brain stem (reptilian brain) and then to the parietal lobes in the cerebral cortex. For instance, when playing baseball, if a pitcher throws an inside fastball about head high, most individuals would instinctively step back or duck to avoid being hit. This reflexive action does not occur on a conscious level, as our older *how* pathway allows us to visually respond to information in an instinctive and survival type of manner before cognitively appreciating the event. In other words, if we were to consciously speculate that a baseball thrown at 90 miles per hour was about to inflict significant damage to our head, we would surely be hit by the ball before having any chance to take some evasive maneuver. Therefore, we react first to the stimulus (older visual pathway), then consciously realize a baseball

(*what* pathway) was thrown at our head (*where* pathway). Lastly, some emotional reaction is then generated once we realize the danger of the circumstance.

The ***temporal lobes*** do not have a unitary function per se, although they play a vital role in housing language and memory functions, as well as processing auditory input and regulating moods and behavior. As noted previously, nearly all right-handers and approximately 70 percent of left-handers have language functions stored in the left temporal lobe. The left temporal lobe, specifically the ***superior temporal gyrus (planum temporale)*** is extremely critical for decoding the 44 phonemes which comprise all the sounds of the English language. In addition, Wernicke's area plays an important role in deciphering language vs. nonlanguage sounds (Kolb & Whishaw, 1996). Therefore, damage to ***Wernicke's area*** tends to be more lexical in nature, while damage to the superior temporal lobe tends to impair actual phoneme recognition (Goldberg & Costa, 1981). With respect to reading, visual information processed in the occipital lobes reaches the temporal lobes for linguistic interpretation via the ***corpus callosum,*** a band of approximately 200 million nerve fibers which bridge the hemispheres. According to Goldberg (1989), visual object agnosia is when there is a disruption of visual association areas interfacing with the temporal lobe region, precluding the identification or recognition of objects by sight. There is no blindness involved, as these individuals can decipher important features of an object; however, the ability to assign a meaningful category to a visual stimulus is lost. For instance, someone looking at a pen might be able to describe its relative shape, size, and color, but be unable to classify the object as pen. Perhaps some children unable to recognize letters or numbers on a consistent basis have another subtype of visual object agnosia.

The ***parietal lobes*** are involved in sensory and tactile functioning as well as visual-spatial orientation. The inferior parietal lobe has been of great interest to cognitive neuroscientists, as this is the region that represents the interface between the occipital, temporal, and parietal lobes. It is referred to collectively as the *posterior tertiary zone*. In essence, many psychologists believe it is the seat of higher level intelligence. It lies in the inferior region of the parietal lobes. With respect to reading, much research has centered on the ***angular gyrus,*** whose chief function is presumed to be involved in mapping visually presented inputs into linguistical representations. The angular gyrus has enormous implications in the study of dyslexia, as this region acts as the conduit or *junction box* for transferring printed information into a linguistically meaningful code, namely, reading. In fact, research using positron emission tomography (PET) has shown that in developmental dyslexia, there appears to be a disconnection between the left angular gyrus and other hemsispheric regions (Horwitz, Rumsey, & Donohue, 1998). As

will be discussed in later chapters, most educators acknowledge that the ability to develop phonemic awareness skills is intrinsically linked to the emergence of successful reading. Interestingly, the **supramarginal gyrus,** which represents the interface between the partietal and temporal lobes, presumably regulates the spatial relations of language (Goldberg, 1989). Hence, damage to this region leads to acalculia, or mathematics disabilities as well as semantic forms of aphasia.

Lastly, the **frontal lobes** occupy more than a third of the brain's cortical surface and remain intimately involved with the highest levels of cortical functioning (Filley, 1995). This region of the brain has been somewhat elusive to measure since the frontal lobes seem to be more involved with how a person utilizes intelligence in a goal directed manner, as opposed to representing intelligence itself. In other words, the frontal lobes, which are the most phylogenetically recent areas of the brain to develop, are analogous to a maestro of an orchestra, while the rest of the brain comprises the band itself. There are three clearly defined regions including the **primary motor cortex,** which controls body movement, the **premotor cortex** which initiates motor movement, and the **prefrontal cortex** or *anterior tertiary zone,* which houses the highest levels of cortical functioning as well as functions governing personality and temperament. A unique aspect of the frontal lobes is the numerous cortical and subcortical interconnections, which allows this region to communicate with the whole brain. A dense array of *association fiber pathways* connect cortical-to-cortical regions while *projection fiber pathways* allow for subcortical-to-cortical communication. Therefore, the frontal lobes organize higher level cognitive processes which allow us to plan for present and future oriented events, strategically shift our behavior to reach designated goals, initiate strategies in pursuit of goals, and transfer newly acquired skills from one situation to another.

With respect to reading, an important region embedded within the premotor cortex lies in **Broca's area (frontal operculum)** believed to be involved with the production of speech. This region appears to be organized somewhat differently in each hemisphere, as the left side is more involved with the production of grammar in language, whereas the right side is involved with prosody of speech and intonation of voice (Kolb & Whishaw, 1996). An important pathway called the **arcuate fasciculus,** a long bundle of white fiber tracts, connects Wernicke's area (receptive language) to Broca's area (production of language). During speech development, children learn how the speech they hear maps onto the sounds they produce. Generally, the anterior and posterior language areas become linked by way of the arcuate fasciculus by approximately 18 months of age, enabling infants to formulate multiword strings (Posner & Raichle, 1994). Successful use of the alphabet depends upon the precise mappings

between individual graphemes, phonemes, and whole word sounds. Damage to the arcuate fasciculus may result in weak mappings connecting the sounds that children hear (Wernicke's area) with the sounds that children produce (Broca's area). Research studies have demonstrated that Broca's area contributes independently to phonological perception, and is particularly active when engaged in rhyming tasks (Paulesu, et. al., 1996). Therefore, the frontal lobes, in particular Broca's area, play a vital role in the developmental reading process. This region completes the language circuitry, and lays down the linguistical foundation for reading. As will be discussed in later sections, the frontal lobes play an important role in the *sustaining* and *focus-execute* parameters of attention while reading (a part of fluency). They also direct *working memory,* which is a complex set of processes that allow for transfer of information from short-term to long-term storage (a part of comprehension).

# Magnocellular Hypothesis

# Chapter 5

The history of dyslexia dates back approximately 100 years, as students who originally demonstrated reading failure in the presence of otherwise normal cognitive functioning were deemed to suffer from *congenital word blindness.* The prevailing view of that time remained that dyslexia involved damage to the part of the brain believed to be important in the visual-memory images of words (Hynd & Cohen, 1983). Interestingly, a popular remediation strategy during this era was to force students to write with their left-hand. This way, the contralateral hemisphere (right hemisphere) could begin to assume language functions that apparently the left hemisphere was unable to master.

In the United States, Samuel Orton contributed a uniquely different perspective regarding the psychological processes believed to be involved with reading. It was conjectured that a student needed to be left-hemispheric dominant, and thus strongly right-handed, to be a proficient reader. Hence, deficient readers were thought to be the result of poor cerebral dominance, and the reversal of letters was a primary characteristic of this lack of hemispheric dominance. Therefore, when students were delayed in establishing a dominant hemisphere, the mirror image of the word was read instead. For instance, the word "saw" was presumed to be represented correctly in the left hemisphere, though was reversed as "was" in its representation in the right hemisphere. Without a left hemispheric dominance for reading, dyslexia was thereby characterized as backwards or mirror reading by the nondominant hemisphere. A key component of Orton's theory was the concept of delayed lateralization, meaning that

most students could eventually be taught to read. This notion was seized upon by educators as a host of remediation strategies were developed to remediate dyslexia based on Orton's insights. By 1953, virtually every state had developed special education programs for children experiencing failure in school. Despite Orton's hypotheses being widely embraced by the educational community, his insights had little to do with our understanding of brain/behavior relationships in dyslexic children (Hynd & Cohen, 1983). Furthermore, children were subjected to ridiculous and often unsuccessful intervention approaches based upon the false notion of cerebral dominance. Some of the more outlandish intervention strategies involved reading with one eye shut, using colored overlays when reading, and improving motor coordination by balancing on a beam in order to develop the necessary interplay between the hemispheres for successful reading to emerge. Today, we find lingering remnants of Orton's model of dyslexia woven into the fabric of pop-psychology, as many psychologists as well as professional educators still regard reading as a visual/spatial deficit characterized by "backwards" reading and written language skills.

Currently, the **magnocellular hypothesis** is a much more sophisticated approach toward explaining dyslexia from primarily a visual deficit point of view. It was postulated that in 75 percent of dyslexic readers the magnocellular pathways, which transmit rapidly changing visual sensations, operate at a somewhat slower pace (Ridder, et. al., 1997). The magnocellular pathway begins in the retina and responds to visual stuimuli based upon motion and contrast sensitivity (Demb, et. al., 1998). The information travels to the lateral geniculate nucleus of the thalamus, then projects back to the occipital lobe for processing. According to this theory, dyslexics have as many as 27 percent fewer neurons in the magnocellular layers than is normal, resulting in much slower visual processing (Livingstone, et.al, 1991). Hence, the magnocellular deficit of reading is more of an "input" type of theory as the underlying factor accounting for reading deficits due to difficulty in rapidly processing visual information in a cohesive fashion. Still, other researchers have speculated the magnocellular system causes reading difficulties through a failure to suppress activity from the neighboring parvocellular system during saccadic eye movements (Lovegrove, 1980). The parvocellular system operates during eye fixations, while the magnocellular system operates during saccades, or rapid eye movements from one fixation to the next, as is the case when reading. Therefore, during reading, it was thought that neural effects from the stimulation of reading one word would carry over into reading the next word on a page, resulting in inconsistent fixations and much confusion.

The magnocellular hypothesis has not been embraced by most neuropsychologists as a suitable explanation for deficits in reading with children. First of all, there has been much inconsistency in the research, and many prominent studies *have not* found evidence for a magnocellular deficit in dyslexia (Victor, 1993). Second, it seems plausible that the magnocellular deficits seen in some children may be the result, and not the cause, of reading failure. Perhaps these children are less skilled in taking in information in a series of rapid eye successions because their reading difficulty has precluded them from engaging in this task. Hence, over time there has been a gradual reduction in the number of visual cells assigned this duty due to a sheer lack of practice. As will be noted in the next chapter, neurons, especially visual neurons, are specifically sensitive to environmental stimuli. When not exposed to a particular stimuli during a given developmental window, neurons tend to die off or become re-routed to assume other functions (Kotulak, 1997). Lastly, the magnocellular hypothesis does not offer a suitable explanation to account for the numerous subtypes of dyslexia. In sum, modern neuroscience would tend to argue against any theory that relied solely on a visual deficit hypothesis to explain developmental dyslexia, as most neuropsychologists agree that dyslexia is primarily a linguistic, and not visual, deficit.

# neural circuitry of reading

# Chapter 6

Until recently, neuroscientists had no sophisticated tools for evaluating a working brain. While magnetic resonance imaging (MRI) and computerized axial tomography (CAT) scans have been available since the 1970s, these instruments only allow us to view structure and not function. Thus, CAT scans and MRIs offer images of a static brain, and though invaluable in detecting clots and tumors, they provide little information on a working brain (Amen, 1997). Since the 1980s, it has become increasingly clear that many neurological problems and psychiatric disorders are not necessarily disorders of the brain's anatomy, but rather problems with functional capability. Today, functional MRIs and positron emission topography (PET) are at the forefront of neuroimaging technologies. These scanning procedures identify brain regions at work during a given cognitive task by measuring activation states. While making up just 2% of our body weight (the average brain weighs approximately 1400g), the human brain uses up to 25% of our oxygen supply and 70% of our glucose to fuel itself. Hence, when neurons become more active, they need more oxygen and glucose and thus require increased blood flow. PET scans produce strikingly clear pictures of the human brain at work by measuring metabolic activity with a radioactive tracer injected into the bloodstream. The outgoing emissions from the isotopes injected into the bloodstream are measured with a computer and indicate oxygen or glucose metabolism. Therefore, the colored portions revealed in PET scans actually show degree to which these regions of the brain are at work during a given cognitive task. PET studies have revolutionized cognitive neuroscience by allowing functional states to be uncovered within the neural architecture of the brain. In essence, chemical changes in the brain can actually be

observed as a result of mental activity. With this technology, a working model of the neural circuitry of reading can begin to be mapped out.

State of the art neuroimaging procedures such as fMRIs, PET scans, and other techniques can capture *real time* brain functions associated with normal reading and reading disorders. Neuropsychological measures in conjunction with neuroimaging techniques will enhance our knowledge and understanding of cognitive deficits as they relate to faulty metabolism. As a result of this merger, there will be more clinical relevance ascribed to the underlying neural circuitry in the left prefrontal region, premotor cortex, Broca's area, and reciprocal metabolic functions in the plana temporale, angular and supramarginal gyri will be better understood.

The working memory contributions to the reading process can be explored through functional neuroimaging deep within the temporal lobes, wherein lies the ***entorhinal cortex*** and ***hippocampus.*** Here, the modulation of the cholinergic neurotransmitter system results in changes with working memory performance, an important component of reading comprehension. With greater enhancement of cholinergic functioning, there can be significantly improved processing efficiency, which ultimately reduces the effort needed to perform a given task. The cortical region known as the entorhinal cortex in conjunction with the hippocampus is responsible for the registration of newly learned information. Another factor crucial to the reading process is the visual system, with its ability to perceive letters and words, and to scan the lines of print. The visual system has known cortical-to-cortical and cortical-to-subcortical pathways that are interconnected through a vast array of association fiber networks and projection fiber networks. The integrity of these networks can be seen through the eyes of functional imaging, which can create a chemical map that enables us to view this process. The fuel intake of glucose or oxygen will reveal the efficacy of these pathways in relation to their functional potential.

Metabolic neuroimaging studies of pathological brains have consistently shown changes in metabolism within discrete brain regions. Lowered metabolic activity is a pathological marker during resting states and pathological increases are seen in metabolism during activation states. When analyzing a task breakdown of the reading process, it is anticipated that reductions or increases in metabolism may result, specifically in the areas of the ***angular gyrus.*** These fluctuations in metabolism represent the interface between the occipital, temporal, and parietal lobes. Interhemispheric asymmetries may also be apparent as well. The effort to find possible alterations in brain metabolism, interdigitated with specific neuropsychological profiles for these individuals, will lead to a more thorough understanding of the reading process,

and to more precise remediation efforts. In essence, understanding the neural substrates linked to these cognitive tasks can be used to assist in treating developmental dyslexia.

In a fascinating series of experiments, Posner & Raichle (1994) have used PET technology to gain a better understanding of the cerebral organization involved in reading. Table 6-1 shows a horizontal view of the brain studying four types of visual codes, and Figure 6-1 illustrates the various brain regions activated during each cognitive task. The first code was enabled *false fonts* and was simply a complex collection of various lines with different spatial organization. Notice that increased metabolic activity in which the right hemisphere is more activated than the left, in particular, the right posterior portion of the brain in the occipital lobe. The second code was labeled *letter-strings* and consisted of actual letters in a random order. Once again, the right hemisphere was particularly active in analyzing the visual features of the stimuli, though deemed these letters as conveying little meaning; therefore, little activation was noted in the left hemisphere. In the third trial labeled *pseudowords,* the consonants and vowels were arranged to reflect the rules of the English language. It should be noted that the *pseudowords* had no meaning. Nevertheless, the *pseudowords* activated both the left and right hemispheres. At one level, the brain recognized the visual features of the stimuli, just like in the previous trials, as noted by activation of the right hemisphere. However, the left hemisphere was also activated as these stimuli appeared to be analyzed according to the orthographic rules of language. Therefore, a definite transfer of information occurs from the right hemisphere to the left via the corpus callosum, in order to determine linguistic meaning from visual stimuli. The final trial consisted of actual words, with primarily the left hemisphere, specifically the left occipital/temporal regions, involved in the analysis.

## TABLE 6-1

| EXAMPLES OF FOUR TYPES OF VISUAL STIMULI |
| --- |

(From *Images of Mind,* by M.I. Posner and M.E. Raichle, p. 79, Copyright 1997 by Scientific American Library. Reprinted with permission of W.H. Freeman and Company.)

| Example of the Four Types of Visual Stimuli | | | |
| --- | --- | --- | --- |
| Words | Pseudowords | Letterstrings | False Fonts |
| ANT | GEEL | USFFHT | AH3 |
| RAZOR | IOB | TBBL | J9JU |
| DUST | RELD | TSTFS | JQPU |
| FURNACE | BLERCE | JBTT | FFDN |
| MOTHER | CHELDINABE | STB | UURJS |
| FARM | ALDOBER | FFPM | EADU |

# FIGURE 6-1

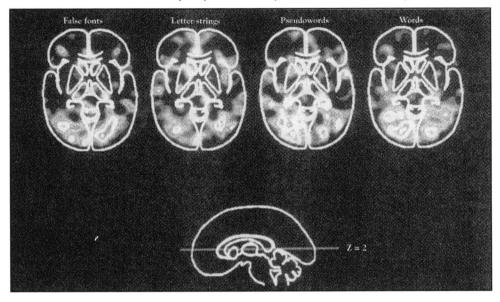

**PET SCAN OF BLOOD FLOW RESPONSES FROM VISUAL STIMULI**

(Adapted from Images of Mind, by M.I. Posner and M.E. Raichle, p. 80, Copyright 1994, Scientific American Library. Reprinted with permission from author.)

A second PET study completed by Posner & Raichle (1994) revealed that there may be a secondary pathway used by the brain to process reading, especially by more proficient readers. A group of 12 college students were scanned under three experimental conditions. First, each student was asked to generate a verb when shown a noun. For instance, if the word *hammer* were shown on a screen, the students might say the word *pound.* The second condition had each student use the same list of nouns, though first practiced generating a verb with each noun for 15 minutes before being scanned. The final condition introduced a new list of nouns. As can be seen by Figure 6-2, the brain has a remarkable capacity to change the areas being used based upon practice. During the initial verb generation task labeled naïve the areas of the brain being activated were the ***anterior cingulate cortex,*** an area of the brain involved in focused attention and registering emotional information, the frontal cortex including ***Broca's area,*** which generates speech, and the ***left temporal cortex,*** which is involved in understanding speech. Also activated was the right ***cerebellum,*** a region normally involved in motor coordination, though it might play a role in the conscious selection of a new skill. During the *practiced* tasks, none of the aforementioned regions were activated.

## fIGURE 6-2

**PET SCAN OF 3 VERTICAL SLICES OF THE BRAIN REVEALING PRACTICE EFFECTS**

(Adapted from Images of Mind, by M.I. Posner and M.E. Raichle, p. 127, Scientific American Library. Copyright 1994 by Oxford University Press. Reprinted with permission.)

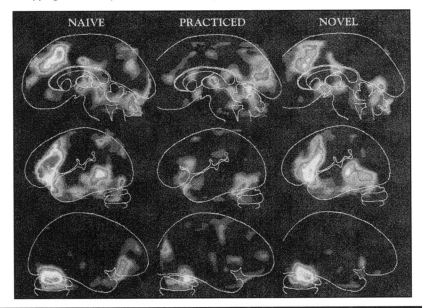

Instead, the insular cortex, buried deep beneath the parietal and temporal lobes, was activated in both hemispheres. Once again, during the third trial in the *novel* task, when an entirely new set of nouns was presented, the same brain regions as in the initial trial were activated. No activation was noted in the insular cortex. The implications of this study suggest that the brain has dual pathways for engaging in the exact same task. During the learning phase of a task, many more brain regions are activated than during a mastery phase of a task. Therefore, it seems plausible to assume that many more regions of the brain are activated during the learning stages of a task such as reading, than during the mastery stages of this task. In other words, the brain operates in very much a reductionistic manner and does not waste important cognitive resources on over-learned tasks. The ***insular cortex*** appears to be the *automatic pilot* of the brain. Perhaps in developmental dyslexia, the brain's automatic pathway, namely the insular cortex, never becomes activated, thereby leaving the process of reading as always a novel task, demanding numerous cognitive resources.

The notion of an inactive insular cortex as a possible explanation for developmental dyslexia was further confirmed in a series of PET studies completed by Paulesu et. al. (1996). In contrast to normal controls, the left insula was never activated for persons with developmental dyslexia, suggesting that the ability to automatically and rapidly scan visual information, namely to read, was processed in a more serial than simultaneous fashion. In other words, persons with dyslexia were able to activate individual sites of the phonological system separately, though were unable to do so simultaneously. For instance, Broca's area was activated in both groups during a rhyming task, and Wernicke's area was activated during a phonemic awareness task. However, these areas were never activated in concert among the dyslexic group, and there were some areas that were consistently activated less than controls. In summary, both the neuropsychological and PET findings point to dyslexia as stemming from a lack of harmony or integrity among the various brain regions needed to process linguistic information from print. The crux of the difficulty appears to be a disconnection between different phonological codes within the neural circuitry of the brain. Therefore, based upon the integrity of the neural circuitry involved with reading, many specific subtypes of dyslexia can be identified.

### TABLE 6-2

**PHONOLOGICAL CIRCUIT OF READING**

**Step 1**  The English language is read from left to right. Visual information projected to primary visual cortex in right occipital lobe.

**Step 2**  Information travels via the corpus callosum to left temporal lobe for phonemic coding (Grapheme/Phoneme analysis).

**Step 3**  Auditory cues are used to decipher word from lexicon by way of angular gyrus and supramarginal gyrus.

**Step 4**  The insular cortex automatizes process to allow for rapid and automatic word recognition. Information is then sent to frontal lobes for output.

**Step 5**  Whole word recognition travels to Broca's area by way of arcuate fasciculus. This completes the articulatory loop and word is read aloud.

In summary, it is critical that school psychologists understand the underlying brain behavior relationships associated with reading disorders, so they can use the neurocognitive data in more useful ways to develop and fine tune Individual Education Plans (IEPs). Another form of treatment for future intervention with the various forms of dyslexia may include specific pharmacological agents that alter synaptic transmission of critical regions that subserve the reading process. Despite many technical developments that allow for more dynamic scanning and better resolution capability, absolute quantification of neuroimaging data for diagnostic purposes still remains problematic with reading. However, some day in the not-so-distant future, cognitive neuroscientists will be able to solve the technical and practical problems confounding these state-of-the art technologies. They will also make the use of neuropsychological test instruments progressively more important in the diagnosing and remediation of dyslexia.

# subtypes of Dyslexia

# Chapter 7

Our earliest records suggest that the ability to synthesize visual codes into meaningful stimuli: namely, to read, has evolved only in the last 5000 to 6000 years. However, one could easily argue that among the 40,000 generations of thinking men and women who preceded us, there existed a more primitive ability to read, and this skill played a vital role in the survival of our species. After all, the ability to read the calendar in the skies dictated when to harvest crops, and reading the position and movement of the sun and the stars predicted when to hunt, when to sow and reap, and when to warn neighboring tribes of danger (Sagan, 1980). Today we find reading as being the single most essential skill necessary for a child to survive in the world of school. The eminent linguist Noam Chomsky and his disciple Steven Pinker have argued persuasively for a *language organ* in the brain, stating that human beings seem pre-wired to acquire language and ultimately literacy. In fact, some estimates have suggested that 75% of children will simply learn to read on their own, 20% of children need to learn reading using a specific methodological procedure, and 5% will never acquire this skill (Mather, 1992). The tools of modern neuroscience have allowed us to look into our own brains and determine how the neural circuitry of reading takes place. Why our brains have evolved to develop such a unique linguistic capability remains a mystery.

The English language consists of 26 letters and 44 phonemes set in a myriad of combinations to produce words (easily producing vocabularies of 10,000 words to upwards of 100,000 words in some). Since English is read in a left to right fashion, the visual input from printed words travel to the lateral geniculate nucleus of the thalamus, and then to the contralateral hemisphere, in this case, the right occipital lobe for processing. Once the information is registered as having the shape, contour, and

syntactic pattern of language, the information travels via the corpus callosum to the left hemisphere for linguistic pattern interpretation. Specifically, the orthographical features of the words are coded in a phonetic manner by the ***superior temporal gyrus,*** or ***planum temporale.*** This is essentially where grapheme/phoneme analysis or *phonics knowledge* takes place. However, it takes more than just *phonics knowledge* or the paired associate of sounds and symbols for successful reading to take place. Phonemic awareness refers to the metacognitive understanding that language sounds are made up of a series of phonemes that occupy a specific temporal order (Clark & Uhry, 1995). This differs from the lower level, paired associate form of learning letters and sounds on a rote level. The next phase of the reading loop involves the inferior portions of the parietal lobes, specifically the ***angular gyrus*** and the ***supramarginal gyrus.*** This region of the brain represents the interface of the occipital, parietal, and temporal lobes, and is heavily involved in mapping linguistic information into functional units (Shaywitz, et. al., 1998). Lastly, whole word recognition travels to Broca's area in the frontal lobes by way of the ***arcuate fasciculus,*** and this completes the articulatory loop and the word is read aloud (Paulesu, et. al., 1996). As mentioned previously, reading at a skilled level involves activation of the insular cortex, and less activation of brain regions involved in segmenting words in a phonological manner. Therefore, reading at a skilled or mastery level involves automatized word recognition, as there is no need to phonetically break down each individual sound while reading. Figure 7-1 illustrates the neural circuitry involved with reading.

## FIGURE 7-1

### NEURAL PATHWAYS INVOLVED IN READING

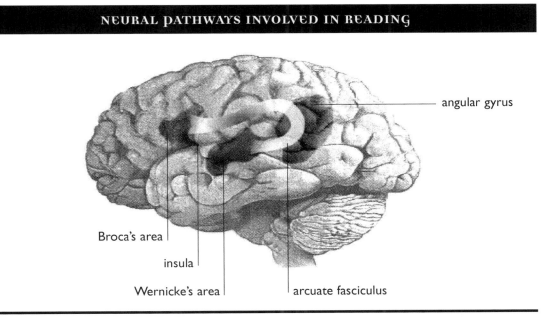

Deviations in the neural circuitry involved with the reading process have allowed neuropsychologists to classify numerous types of reading disorders. Approximately two-thirds of children with a reading disorder are ***dysphonetic*** readers, and have difficulty processing information through auditory channels. This is a basic phonological processing disorder affecting both reading and spelling. In essence, these children have poor decoding skills, and the essential features of sound/symbol associations have not been mastered. Consequently, ***dysphonetic*** readers over-rely on their sight vocabulary to generate *visual images* of words, and have extreme difficulty reading nonwords or words that are phonetically inconsistent (McCarthy & Warrington, 1990). The anatomical region chiefly responsible for grapheme/phoneme analysis is the superior temporal gyrus or planum temporale. An error analysis of dysphonetic readers might include difficulty with the following words:

TABLE 7-1

| ERROR ANALYSIS OF DYSPHONETIC DYSLEXIA | |
| --- | --- |
| **Same Sound/Different Spelling** | **Irregular Words** |
| A**ye** | Listen |
| B**uy** | Debt |
| B**y** | Psychology |
| D**ie** | Sword |

There has been compelling evidence that actual structural formations exist in the dyslexic brain due to an increase in symmetry between the hemispheres. As noted in Chapter II, the hemispheres of the brain are not symmetrical, as the left temporal lobe is generally somewhat larger than the right temporal lobe, presumably to house our language functions. In a study by Geschwind & Galaburda (1985), 65% of dyslexic brains showed symmetrical temporal lobes and 11% actually had the right temporal lobe being larger than the left. Operating under the assumption that asymmetry was a natural evolutionary consequence of hemispheric specializations, many researchers proposed that deviations in normal patterns of brain asymmetry was at the core of developmental dyslexia (Hynd, et. al, 1989, & Hynd et. al., 1991). Some have even speculated that high levels of fetal testosterone actually retard the rate of development of the left hemisphere; therefore, brain symmetry actually reflects cellular loss in the left hemisphere (Flowers, 1993). Perhaps this is why left-handedness, good math skills (both presumably controlled by the right hemisphere) and in some cases allergies, often co-occur with dyslexia.

Interestingly, asymmetry of the planum temporale is visible already at 31 weeks of fetal age (Galaburda, et. al, 1990). According to Hynd et al. (1995), deviations in the development of the cerebral cortex generally occurs between the fifth and seventh month of fetal development due to a general growth spurt in brain weight. This is characterized by the development of the various gyri and sulci of the brain, and once this general pattern is laid out, it remains fairly constant. Thus, deviations in the plana temporale are visible at this time, lending credence to the possibility of actually detecting a learning disability prenatally.

Hynd et. al (1995) also looked at the role of the corpus callosum in dyslexia since this bundle of 200 million nerve fibers acts as the main conduit for information to be communicated between the hemispheres. Using MRI procedures, it was noted that the genu of the corpus callosum was significantly smaller in dyslexic children. Consequently, developmental dyslexia may be associated with subtle deviations in the morphology of the corpus callosum preventing efficient interhemispheric communication. This finding seemed consistent with the fact that children born without a corpus callosum have extreme difficulty reading words in a phonological manner. Therefore, dysphonetic dyslexia may be attributed to actual deviations in the plana temporale, or perhaps reflects a break in the neural circuitry as orthographic information has difficulty crossing over into the left hemisphere for phonological processing to commence.

*Surface dyslexia* represents approximately 14 percent of reading disabilities, and is characterized by difficulty visualizing words in a fashion where reading becomes automatic. Consequently, these readers are slower paced, tend to over-rely on sound/symbol associations, and make errors on frequently encountered words. In other words, these types of readers tend to break every word down in a phonetic manner, and reading never becomes an automatic, fluid type of process. Words are painstakingly broken down to individual phonemes and read very slowly and laboriously. These children tend to make errors on frequently encountered words since there is a need to break every word down to its phonological core. While phonological processing is critical to early reading development, skilled readers rely heavily on the ability to automatically recognize words based upon the contour of shapes. An error analysis of surface dyslexia would consist of the following:

TABLE 7-2

| ERROR ANALYSIS OF SURFACE DYSLEXIA | |
| --- | --- |
| **Word** | **Read As** |
| Island | Izland |
| Grind | Grinned |
| Listen | Liston |
| Begin | Beggin |
| Lace | Lake |

Following Luria's model, Goldberg (1989) reasoned that reading and writing deficits occur due to the disintegration of the visual and spatial representations at the highest levels of our brains. Luria postulated primary, secondary, and tertiary areas within each lobe of our brain, with the tertiary area representing higher cortical functioning (Goldberg, 1989). Since surface dyslexia over-relies on the phonetic analysis of words, it seems plausible to assume that this type of dyslexia represents a breakdown of the visual/spatial component of the reading neural circuitry; namely, the angular gyrus. In other words, the tertiary area of the occipital lobe (processing vision) and the tertiary area of the parietal lobe (processing spatial awareness) intersect at the junction in the inferior parietal region called the **angular gyrus.** It is this region of the brain that processes visual/spatial functioning at the highest cortical level.

The visual/spatial synthesis of words, or what is sometimes referred to as **orthographic processing,** appears to have two primary functions. The first allows for the actual synthesis of visual shapes and features of letters and words, and their subsequent memory store. The second is the automatic and rapid perception of whole words by shape, presumably once learned by phonetically sounding them out, so that fluent reading can take place. Therefore, breakdowns in the neural circuitry of reading along the angular gyrus might prevent the automatic and rapid recognition of words; thereby forcing students to over-rely on the phonetic properties of words in order to determine meaning from print. Consequently, these readers painstakingly sound out each phoneme, and never seem to be able to rapidly blend the sounds into a cohesive sound pattern for rapid recognition. As mentioned previously (Chapter VI), there appears to be a dual circuitry for reading, one pathway for beginning readers, and a second pathway for more skilled readers. Since reading at a skilled level also involves activation of the insular cortex, and less activation of brain regions involved in segmenting words in a phonological manner, surface dyslexics may also have difficulty

due to a deactivation of the insular cortex and an over-activation of other brain regions involved in phonological processing (Paulesu, et.al, 1996).

A third form of dyslexia can be classified under the heading of *mixed dyslexia,* as this involves reading and spelling disorders characteristic of both *dysphonetic* and *visual spatial* dysfunction. These children often become severely impaired learners, as there is no usable key to decipher the reading and spelling code. Most agree that skilled readers rely on an interactive system that taps <u>both</u> phonological and visual memory stores simultaneously. This type of reading deficit often involves multiple breakdowns along the neural circuitry for reading, and is characterized by very bizarre error patterns and poor syllabic representation. For instance, an error analysis of mixed dyslexia might include the following:

TABLE 7-3

| ERROR ANALYSIS OF MIXED DYSLEXIA | |
| --- | --- |
| **Word** | **Read As** |
| Advice | Exvices |
| Correct | Corexs |
| Violin | Vilen |
| Museum | Musune |
| Possession | Persessuve |
| Material | Mitear |

According to Bakker (1992), reading and spelling are most strongly associated with right hemisphere activity during the first two years of initial reading. The orthographic features of letters and words are recognized by their visual contour, shape, and size consistency. However, by the end of first grade there is a rapid shift toward left hemispheric activity after the initial phase. With left hemispheric control comes the phonological awareness, syntactical analysis, and semantic cueing which dictates more advanced stages of reading. Similarly, Goldberg & Costa (1981) noted that in the early stages of any task acquisition, the right hemisphere should show superiority in performance, but as the skills necessary for the execution of a task are acquired and routinized, the left hemisphere should eventually gain superiority. This progression seems especially true for language related tasks. Therefore, the instruction of reading should progress from learning letters and matching upper and lower case letters (visual synthesis), and even introducing basals (whole word recognition books) in preschool

and kindergarten, towards a more phonological and linguistic analysis of words in first grade. The concept of hemispheric shifting based upon the specific strategy used to identify words may be at the forefront of mixed dyslexia. Some studies have suggested that the *genu* of the corpus callosum is much smaller in dyslexic children, thus preventing an appropriate transfer of information between the hemispheres (Hynd, et al, 1995). Other studies have shown that the *splenium* portion of the corpus callosum is actually larger in dyslexic children, perhaps preventing the natural asymmetry of language functions (Duara et. al., 1991, Beaton, 1997). While the debate continues, there does seem to be compelling evidence that the morphology of the corpus callosum may be related to dyslexia since this is the anatomical bridge which allows each hemisphere to speak to the other. Furthermore, mixed dyslexia may also represent multiple breakdowns along the neural circuitry of reading, and reflects a lack of functional integrity of the circuit as opposed to just a single deficit area.

Lastly, *deep dyslexia* is a rare form of reading comprehension disorder characterized by impairments in reading words with abstract meanings, but reading more concrete, easily imagined words remain intact (McCarthy & Warrington, 1990). This has often been called a *double deficit* type of reading disorder manifested by poor sound/symbol relationships and difficulty relying solely on the visual contour of letters. Since there is impairment primarily in the phonological route to word recognition, and secondarily in the visual/spatial route to word recognition, the child has no other course of action than to rely on semantic cues to determine meaning from print. Therefore, words which are easily imagined and conjour up a meaningful image, such as nouns like *"table"*, *"chair"*, *"book"*, etc., are read much more efficiently than more abstract words or smaller words which cannot be easily imagined such as *"is"*, *"was"* or *"because"*. Semantic errors are generally the hallmark of this disorder, and an error analysis would consist of the following:

## TABLE 7-4

| ERROR ANALYSIS OF DEEP DYSLEXIA | |
|---|---|
| **Semantic Miscues** | **Visual Miscues** |
| Dinner . . . . . . . . . . . . . . . . Food | Stock . . . . . . . . . . . . . . . . . Shock |
| Occasion . . . . . . . . . . . . . . Event | Crowd . . . . . . . . . . . . . . . . Crown |
| Cemetery . . . . . . . . . . . . . Burial | Grew . . . . . . . . . . . . . . . . . Green |
| Watch . . . . . . . . . . . . . . . . Clock | Saucer . . . . . . . . . . . . . . . Sausage |
| Giggle . . . . . . . . . . . . . . . . Laugh | Bead . . . . . . . . . . . . . . . . . Bread |

There is much speculation over where exactly the breakdown lies in the functional neural circuitry of deep dyslexia. Clearly, these readers have difficulty with grapheme/phoneme analysis, suggesting possible dysfunction of the planum temporale and angular gyrus. However, the type of semantic error pattern suggests difficulty accessing certain words in the lexicon, and since this error pattern is often seen in Broca's aphasia, cortical dysfunction in the prefrontal lobes may be implicated as well (Matthews, 1991). Clearly, deep dyslexia represents multiple breakdowns along the neural circuitry of reading, with very specific error patterns noted.

However, deep dyslexia also sheds much insight into the types of cues necessary to retrieve information from the lexicon. There appears to be three primary cues used to decipher word meanings. For instance, most students may not recognize the word *reconnaissance,* which means a preliminary survey or mission often used in the military to gain information. An unfamiliar word such as this would be broken down into its four recognizable phonemes: *re - conn - ais - sance,* and based upon this phonetic analysis, these sounds would be blended together until a recognizable word form emerged. This is commonly referred to as **auditory cueing.** However, if the word *reconnaissance* reappeared in the next paragraph, there would be no need to once again break the word down into its recognizable phonetic base, but rather the visual structure of the word would cue us to its meaning since this word was just encountered. This is referred to as **visual cueing,** and generally words that can be retrieved visually have also been stored on an auditory level as well. For some, the word *reconnaissance* may be difficult to conceptualize in an auditory format, and the only viable means to recognize the word would be within the context of a sentence. This is referred to as **semantic cueing,** and generally words stored in just a semantic format cannot be recognized in isolation, though they can be recognized by their meaning within the context of a sentence. In deep dyslexia, words tend to be stored by either visual or semantic means, and thus, access to the lexicon of words can only be derived using these strategies. A summary of the cues which aid in comprehension are as follows:

## TABLE 7-5

| SUMMARY OF CUES FOR READING COMPREHENSION |
|---|
| Dysphonetic Dyslexia . . . . . . . . . . . . . . . . . Rely on visual cues |
| Surface Dyslexia . . . . . . . . . . . . . . . . . . . Rely on auditory cues |
| Mixed Dyslexia . . . . . . . . . . . . . . . . . . . . Rely on semantic cues |
| Deep Dyslexia . . . . . . . . . . . . . . . . . . . . . Rely on visual and semantic cues |

There are numerous other types of dyslexias and language disturbances that manifest from deviations along the basic neural circuitry of reading. It is not within the scope of this book to analyze the myriad of difficulties associated with reading or related language types of disorders. As Flowers (1993) noted:

*"The brain is a highly interactive organ with many regions working together to accomplish its functions. It is not hard to imagine a task as complex as reading to involve more than one sensory system, including an optimal level of arousal, organization and execution of a motor response, attentional control, working memory, and long-term memory, all working together in a simultaneous and cohesive fashion. (Flowers, p. 577)"*

Nevertheless, some of the lower incidence types of dyslexias include the following:

a) ***Hyperlexia*** - The uncanny ability to decode words despite significant cognitive deficiencies. Comprehension is often very poor, though decoding and spelling skills are well developed.
   ***Anatomical Explanation*** - Phonological loop of brain intact, specifically the region along the left superior temporal gyrus in spite of damage in other brain regions.

b) ***DeJerine Syndrome*** - Dyslexia without dysgraphia. The child has little difficulty writing, though cannot read. Also known as ***word form dyslexia,*** as the child can identify words if letters are spelled aloud (auditory input) as opposed to identifying words from print.
   ***Anatomical Explanation*** - Disconnection of visual input to auditory cortex via the corpus callosum. In other words, there is a break in the neural circuitry, preventing information to travel from the occipital lobe (visual input) to the temporal lobe (linguistic processing), though information presented in an auditory format can be deciphered since this information goes directly to the temporal lobes.

c) ***Neglect Dyslexia*** - An inability to read words on the left side of the page. Usually not a developmental dyslexia, but rather acquired due to a head injury or some type of cerebral insult.
   ***Anatomical Explanation*** - Often lesions on the right parietal lobe disrupt the brain's ability to perceive and identify information from the contralateral side (left side).

d) ***Wernicke's Dyslexia*** - The inability to comprehend written material despite adequate intelligence and word identification skills.
   ***Anatomical Explanation*** - Damage to Wernicke's area in the left temporal lobes produces receptive aphasia. Not only does a student have difficulty understanding oral language, but also cannot comprehend written material as well.

# The 90 Minute Dyslexia Evaluation

# Chapter 8

The field of psychology is fraught with classification systems in a never ending attempt to simplify and categorize the realm of possibilities which human behavior may take. The psychological world has become inundated with 12-step recovery programs, 7-step secrets to successful management, and personality typology ranging from 16 trait specific types to the 12 astrological signs based upon the arrangement of the stars. But the truth is that there are no simple formulas, no quick fixes, and no pre-packaged programs that produce meaningful and enduring changes in our cognitive and emotional make-up. Human beings are so biologically complex and constantly in a state of flux, that at any moment the maps of our brains may change as we learn new information or experience new events. In other words, the brain has the capacity to rearrange its 500 trillion or so connections in response to incoming stimuli or just by merely triggering a thought from within (Kotulak, 1997). Consider this: at any one mating, one male and one female could produce 52 trillion biologically distinct individuals (Ornstein, 1993). From this myriad of biological predispositions, the human brain is more susceptible to environmental influences than any other species' brain on the planet. Unlike other species, the human brain weighs 25% of its adult weight at birth, leaving much room for environmental events to shape and mould future neural connections to complete its growth cycle (Chase, 1996). This can be compared to a chimpanzee's brain that is 46% of its adult weight, or that of a fish that is 95% of its adult weight. While other animals are forced to depend on instinct to rule their day-to-day behavior, leaving little room for the environment to shape their remaining brain growth, human beings are in a unique position to depend on conscious experience from their environment to enrich the

connectivity in the brain's neural wiring. Given such an infinite array of possibilities, it is virtually impossible to devise just one systemic classification procedure to assess dyslexia, because the brain is constantly changing and reorganizing itself during critical periods of development, leaving no two brains alike.

The assessment of dyslexia using a neuropsychological paradigm presumes the brain processes language and literacy in a fairly predictable fashion, though assumes the anatomical location of these brain regions may certainly change among individuals. Therefore, the key term in the identification of dyslexia in children is ***integrity*** (not discrepancy) of the functional connectivity and neural circuitry of reading. There is no need to rely on just a simplistic discrepancy formula between aptitude and achievement (see Chapter II) to categorize children as being disabled. Notwithstanding, a basic outlay of some of the assessment instruments that can be used to identify the integrity of the neural circuitry involved with reading are illustrated. By no means is this considered a comprehensive or exhaustive list of instruments to use, but merely a sampling. The model is flexible enough to be used in a developmental fashion to identify reading disorders as early as in kindergarten, and succinct enough for any school psychologist to complete in a single session.

## 90 MINUTE DYSLEXIA EVALUATION

1. **Intelligence:**
   - Evaluate WISC III in terms of level of performance as well as patterns of performance.
   - Cognitive Assessment System for in-depth processing
2. **Phonological Awareness:**
   - Word Attack subtest of Woodcock-Johnson
   - Accuracy subtest from Gray-Oral Reading Test
   - Phonological Processing & Nonsense Words from NEPSY
   - Phonological Awareness Test (Robertson & Salter)
   - Comprehensive Test of Phonological Processing (C-TOPP)
   - Process Assessment of the Learner (PALS)
   - Lindamood Auditory Conceptualization Test (LAC)
3. **Rapid Naming Tests:**
   - Verbal Fluency & Speeded Naming from NEPSY
   - Controlled Oral Word Association (COWA) "FAS" test
   - Process Assessment of the Learner (PALS)
   - Rapid Automatized Naming Tests (Denckla)
   - Comprehensive Test of Phonological Processing (C-TOPP)
4. **Verbal Memory Tests:**
   - Test of Memory and Learning (TOMAL)
   - Children's Memory Scales (CMS)
   - California Verbal Learning Test
   - Rey Auditory Verbal Learning Test
   - Comprehension of Instructions from NEPSY
   - WRAML
5. **Naming Subtests:**
   - Body Part Naming & Verbal Fluency from NEPSY
   - Picture naming from the K-BIT
   - Expressive One Word Vocabulary Test
   - Aphasia Screening Test from Halstead-Reitan Battery
   - Boston Naming Test
6. **Visual Spatial Skills:**
   - Visuospatial processing subtests from NEPSY
   - Jordan Left Right Reversal Test
   - Bender Gestalt
   - Beery Visual Motor Integration Test

- Nonverbal Matrices: Cognitive Assessment System
- Rey-Osterrieth Complex Figure Test

**7. Set Shifting and Attention:**
- Trailmaking Test/Stroop Test
- Wisconsin Card Sort Test
- Cognitive Assessment System: Planning Subtests

**8. Family History**

*Intelligence:* There is no question that assessing a child's general intellectual ability provides vital information on the cognitive strengths and weaknesses a student possesses in any given learning situation. Unfortunately, most paradigms focusing on intelligence do so from a level of performance approach only, and overlook many underlying variables that highlight how a child processes information. According to Reitan & Wolfson (1992) and reiterated by Jarvis & Barth (1994), there are four ways to interpret testing data from a neuropsychological perspective: 1) Level of performance, 2) Patterns of performance, 3) Right-left hemispheric functioning, and 4) Pathognomonic signs. The WISC III remains an excellent predictor of school success, though relying solely on a Full Scale IQ score to describe an enigmatic concept such as intelligence is not only misleading, but also does a disservice to children by classifying them into arbitrary categories. Patterns of performance comparing visual versus verbal tasks, timed versus untimed subtest performance, and crystallized vs. fluid reasoning measures provide rich clinical information to describe how a child learns best. Lastly, specific pathognomonic signs such as processing speed, attention and concentration, and sensory perceptual functioning should be evaluated as well. There is no single test score that is pathognomonic of dyslexia, but rather dyslexia should reflect a thoughtful synthesis of all the clinical data available (Shaywitz, 1998). Therefore, intelligence tests should be interpreted in a more *process-oriented* format instead of relying solely on a *level of performance* approach in order to break down the cognitive strengths and weaknesses of a learner.

*Phonological Awareness Tests:* There is overwhelming evidence in the literature that a primary cause of variability among children in early word reading skills involves individual differences in the ability to process the phonological features of language (Torgesen & Hecht, 1996). In the school age child, the most important element of the psychometric evaluation of dyslexia is how accurately a child can decode words (Shaywitz, 1998). Countless studies have shown that the single best predictor of reading difficulty in kindergarten and first grade is phonological awareness, and not intelligence test scores (Hurford, et. al, 1994, Lyon, 1996). Knowledge of the alphabetic code allows

children to independently use linguistic and auditory cues to break down unfamiliar words. There appear to be two distinct forms of phonological processing which need to be teased out in the evaluation process. The first involves just rote level phonics that involves pairing an isolated sound with a symbol. From a neuropsychological perspective, this involves the functional integrity of the *plana temporale* in the left hemisphere to successfully classify sound patterns with symbols. The second type is more of a higher level phonemic awareness skill which includes a range of higher level metacognitive understandings of word boundaries, syllable boundaries, and isolating and segmenting phonemes within a given word (Clark & Uhry, 1995). Some of the tests included might involve rhyming activities, sound blending, sound segmenting, and reading and decoding nonwords. It should be noted that many of these tests take less than 15 minutes to administer. According to Lyon (1996), phonics and phonemic awareness testing can predict with 90% accuracy kindergarten students who will have reading difficulty in later grades. However, mastery of phonemic awareness does not equate to mastery of the reading process. From a neuropsychological standpoint, phonemic awareness involves more of the reading neural circuitry and includes the angular gyrus. It should be noted that in later grades, remnants of a poor phonological base are often noted in spelling, which is why an error analysis of a student's writing sample is often a necessity with these students.

***Rapid Naming Tests:*** Naming is an important subcomponent of language, and reflects the automaticity with which information can be accessed and retrieved from the lexicon. Word-finding problems may be secondary to a more generalized language disorder, though Denkla & Rudel (1976) demonstrated that children with reading problems were slower than good readers on tasks of automatic naming of letters, numbers, colors, and familiar objects. In essence, rapid naming appears to provide a global measure of the overall functional integrity of the neural circuitry involved with reading. As noted previously, Wolf (1999) suggested that naming speed was a better predictor of reading difficulty than IQ or phonological awareness, especially in more orthographically regular languages such as German, Dutch, Finnish, and Spanish. In addition, rapid naming tests yield important information toward how information is stored in the lexicon. For instance, students with deep dyslexia tend to over-rely on semantic cues to determine meaning from print. Therefore, naming as many animals or as many foods as possible in one minute should be a relatively simple task. However, naming as many words that start with the letter *"f"* or the letter *"s"*, a task necessitating the storage and retrieval of information in a phonological (by letter) manner, may prove to be much more difficult.

***Verbal Memory Tests:*** The ability to encode information, store it, and at a later time, retrieve information from storage is one of the most complex cognitive functions and requires a host of perceptual processing functions. Reading comprehension depends heavily upon ***semantic*** memory, the registration of facts encoded and stored primarily in the temporal lobes, yet accessed by the frontal lobes (Carter, 1998). Generally, auditory information of a linguistic form is processed in the left temporal lobe, an area that is vital in the neural circuitry of reading. Verbal learning and memory tests provide important information on preferred learning strategies as well as attention and concentration to auditory stimuli. However, the human memory system is very difficult to quantify, due in part to the sheer selectivity of the system. Items of interest, something that varies from individual to individual, are retained much better than dry facts. From a biological standpoint, memories themselves are groups of neurons that fire together in the same pattern each time they are activated (Carter, 1998). Since auditory verbal memories are housed in similar brain regions to those which house the neural circuitry of language, important information about the functional integrity of this region can be ascertained through these types of tests.

***Naming Subtests:*** The ability to attach a verbal tag to a visual stimulus provides much insight into the integrity of the neural connections necessary for reading to emerge. Before a developing nervous system can be expected to match a grapheme with a phoneme, a more rudimentary form of visual/verbal interaction needs to take place. The efficacy with which a student can name objects reveals an intact ***ventral stream,*** which means that there is an appropriate transfer of information from the occipital lobe to the temporal lobe via the corpus callosum for meaningful classification and recognition to occur. In fact, visual object agnosia is a syndrome characterized by the dissociation between an intact visual sensory system and an impaired ability to assign a visual stimulus to a category to determine its meaning (Goldberg, 1989). Sometimes referred to as *tip of the tongue* phenomena, a student might see a picture of a *pen,* describe its shape, its color, and perhaps gesture as to its function, though be unable to classify the object as a pen. Many studies have looked at the key predictors in kindergarten that can accurately differentiate skilled vs. unskilled readers in later grades. Badian et. al. (1990) identified naming and phonological awareness tests in kindergarten as being the key predictors in differentiating students with dyslexia from normal readers in fourth grade with 98% accuracy. As Wolf (1999) noted:

*"Naming speed represents ensembles of multiple perceptual, lexical, and motoric processes, all of the subprocesses of which must function smoothly and rapidly in order to produce a verbal match for an abstract, visually presented symbol (p. 12)."*

***Visual/Spatial Skills:*** The majority of visual/spatial reasoning and processing occurs in the right occipital/parietal regions of the brain, outside the primary neural pathways normally associated with reading and language. Despite the popular notion in our culture that dyslexia stems from seeing backwards letters, the overwhelming evidence from the neuropsychological literature suggests dyslexia is a linguistic, not a spatial, deficit. In fact, visual perceptual training has been proven ineffective in improving reading skills with dyslexic children (Bateman, 1979). Nevertheless, a brief evaluation of visual perceptual functioning can provide useful clinical information when evaluating children. In addition, certain low incidence types of dyslexias, such as *neglect dyslexia,* obvious pathognomonic signs, and other important neurological variables can be ascertained. Certainly, students with visual perceptual difficulties may have difficulty visually tracking words on a page, or struggle to accurately identify words and letters.

***Set Shifting and Attention:*** Virtually any skill as complex as reading involves an integration of numerous brain regions including an elusive domain known as **executive functioning.** This refers to the brain's ability to initiate, shift, organize, focus, and self-monitor while engaged in a particular task, and often implicates the prefrontal lobes. Executive functioning is a convenient term that encapsulates a host of psychological attributes necessary to perform a task at peak efficiency. In the developmental progression of reading, comprehension of extended language requires active organization of incoming information. In other words, as children scan across each word within the context of a sentence, there is a need to temporarily suspend recently processed information in memory in order to focus on the next incoming word or phrase. This information is then paired with previously stored material so that meaningful comprehension can take place. The ability to change sets, or shift attention from an upcoming word or phrase to the previously read word or phrase to derive some conceptual meaning from the passage itself requires flexible executive functioning skills. Therefore, measures of executive functioning become more and more essential with children who have reading comprehension difficulties. According to Shaywitz (1991), somewhere between 10 and 20 percent of children with dyslexia also have an attention-deficit disorder. Perhaps the core deficiency with both dyslexic children and some types of attention-deficit-disorder lies in a faulty executive functioning system within the neural pathways that modulates these skills.

***Family History:*** Clinicians have long been convinced that dyslexia runs in families. Research carried out as part of the Colorado twin study indicated that in 70 percent of the cases with identical twins, when one twin had a reading disorder, the other did as well. However, with fraternal twins, the concordance rate was only about 48 percent (DeFries et. al., 1991). Interestingly, this study suggested that there was a strong genetic

influence on phonological skills, though this was not the case with orthographic skills. These researchers concluded that dyslexia is both *familial,* with approximately 40% of first degree relatives affected, and also *heritable* with a transmission rate of approximately 50%. Further studies have focused on a possible dyslexia gene, with chromosome 6 and chromosome 15 being possible candidates. However, this research is still in its infancy, and to date, no specific gene for dyslexia has been found. In any event, there appears to be a genetic factor in dyslexia, and as is the case with virtually any psychological evaluation, a detailed developmental history remains essential.

## TABLE 8-1

### DEVELOPMENTAL GUIDELINES FOR ASSESSING DYSLEXIA

**Under Age 7:** While IQ tests certainly yield useful information, they should not be interpreted from a *level of performance* perspective, but rather should be used as a tool to determine how young children process information. Thus, aptitude/achievement discrepancies should be disregarded, and emphasis should be placed on phonological awareness tests, rapid naming tests, and verbal memory. Also, knowledge of parental history of reading deficits is vital.

**Ages 7–12:** Aptitude/Achievement discrepancies certainly have some merit at this age, but should not be used as a necessary or sufficient condition for a child to be labeled as dyslexic. As Mather (1992) pointed out, 75 percent of children should have some mastery over the reading process at this age no matter what the methodology of reading instruction. However, approximately 20 percent of students may need a particular reading methodology to achieve success. Lastly, approximately 5 percent of students may never read at a functional level as they have no usable key to unlock the phonetic code. When evaluating these students, emphasis should be placed on exposure to reading instruction as well as the aforementioned processing deficits. In addition, temperament and personality variables should be addressed.

**Over Age 12:** The primary emphasis when evaluating secondary students should be on reading fluency and comprehension. Attentional and emotional issues can severely impact comprehension, in addition to memory and metacognitive deficits. As stated previously, students who have not mastered the phonological code at this age may never do so. Particular emphasis should be placed on executive function types of issues.

# case studies

# Chapter 9

Two case studies were chosen to illustrate the clinical utility, flexibility, and overall depth of the 90-minute dyslexia model. Once again, this is a ***process-oriented*** approach that evaluates reading disorders in children based upon brain/behavior relationships and the neural circuitry of reading. Unlike a fixed battery approach, which forces the examiner to use a specific research instrument or set of instruments (i.e. Halstead-Reitan Neuropsychological Battery) regardless of the presenting concern, a process oriented or flexible battery approach allows for the picking and choosing of various subtests to tap specific domains of interest. Therefore, tests can be administered based upon referral questions and concerns, and there is no need to rigidly measure cognitive domains that have no bearing on the referral question. It should be noted that the complexity of any psychological evaluation varies; hence, 90 minutes refers to the ***minimal*** amount of time needed to complete a dyslexia evaluation. As the first case illustrates, many referrals require additional hypothesis formulation and investigation, and thus require more time to complete. However, given the time demands of most school psychologists, the 90-minute dyslexia evaluation should sufficiently provide more clinical coverage, greater insight and remediation strategies, and be far more accurate and precise then spending 90 minutes seeking aptitude/achievement discrepancies.

# <u>RICHARD</u>

***Case #1:*** Richard was referred for a dyslexia evaluation due to continued difficulty acquiring and retaining basic reading skills. Assessment was administered in order to determine his future educational needs.

## <u>TESTS ADMINISTERED:</u>
Wechsler Intelligence Scale for Children-III (WISC-III)
Bender Visual-Motor Gestalt Test
Jordan Left-Right Reversal Test
Gray Oral Reading Test - 3rd Edition (GORT-3)
NEPSY: Selected Subtests
California Verbal Learning Test-Children's Version
Wide Range Assessment of Memory and Learning (WRAML)
Piers-Harris Children's Self Concept Test

**<u>BACKGROUND INFORMATION:</u>** Richard is a 12 year-old student currently in the 6th grade at White Oak Middle School. He was referred for a complete dyslexia evaluation due to continued difficulty acquiring and retaining basic reading skills. According to his special education teacher, Richard historically makes measurable progress in reading and written language skills, though often plateaus for a period followed by substantial decline. His overall reading skills were estimated as being on approximately a 2nd grade level despite numerous interventions by the school. For instance, he received daily special education service, in addition to daily drill and practice in reading through the school's alpha-phonics program. This incorporates a multi-sensory approach to decoding words and learning basic sound/symbol associations. According to his alpha phonics-teacher, Richard continued to struggle to identify certain letters of the alphabet, and tended to make semantic substitution errors, such as reading "giggle" for "laugh". His teacher indicated that Richard had difficulty decoding smaller words such as "it", and at times, identified words more efficiently when spelled aloud as opposed to reading them. He reportedly was on approximately a 4th grade level in math, and was described as making frequent number reversals while still learning his multiplication tables. There were concerns expressed by both of his teachers regarding Richard's negative attitude and constant avoidance of reading, in addition to his lack of motivation in school.

**DEVELOPMENTAL HISTORY:** A review of Richard's educational and developmental records indicated no prenatal or postnatal medical complications at birth. Most developmental milestones were reached within normal limits save for speech acquisition. Richard was extremely slow developing independent language, and was evaluated by the White Oak Development Center when he was two and a half years old. The test results indicated a mild delay with expressive language skills, and continued language stimulation at home was recommended. Richard began speaking consistently by age three, though was reevaluated at age 4 due to poor speech intelligibility. Testing indicated both his receptive and expressive language skills, as well as his hearing, were within normal limits. However, Richard qualified for speech and language therapy due to poor articulation skills.

Richard attended preschool prior to beginning kindergarten at White Oak Elementary School. He was referred for a complete psychological evaluation while in kindergarten. At the time, there were concerns regarding his inconsistent school performance, and difficulty with paper and pencil tasks. The test results indicated his overall cognitive abilities were in the *Average* range of functioning *(WPPSI = 90),* with difficulties noted on more visual perceptual types of tasks. Richard then transferred to a neighboring school district and repeated kindergarten. He was reevaluated due to concerns regarding his difficulty acquiring pre-reading and writing skills. His overall cognitive abilities were once again in the *Average* range, though unlike his previous evaluation, his nonverbal problem solving skills were now somewhat better developed than his verbal abilities. Further testing noted both auditory and visual perceptual deficits. Richard qualified for special educational services as a learning disabled student.

He continued to make little educational progress the following year, and was referred for a Central Auditory Processing evaluation toward the end of 2$^{nd}$ grade. The test results indicated a significant delay, meaning Richard had difficulty processing information when a competing message, such as background noise, was present. His special education services were increased to maximum intensity levels for both 3$^{rd}$ and 4$^{th}$ grades. Richard continued to receive speech and language services as well. His most recent psychological evaluation from 4$^{th}$ grade indicated his overall cognitive abilities were in the *Average* range *(FSIQ=95),* with his verbal skills now being much better developed *(VIQ = 102)* than his nonverbal abilities *(PIQ = 89).* Further testing indicated a severe discrepancy between his reading and written language skills, as he was reportedly working on approximately a beginning 1$^{st}$ grade level. The IEP team recommended an intense remedial reading and writing program based upon the Orton-Gillingham approach. Richard continued to have little academic success and was

recommended for summer school services in the form of one-on-one instruction with Project Read. He transferred back to White Oak Elementary School for 5th grade.

Currently, Richard lives at home with his mother and one older brother. Both of his parents are in education as his father is a principal, while his mother teaches elementary school. There was a history of learning difficulty reported on his father's side. Richard indicated he enjoyed school, though admitted to disliking any tasks involving reading.

**TEST RESULTS AND INTERPRETATIONS:** Richard was administered the *WISC-III* in order to assess his overall level of cognitive functioning. This test measures two unique styles of information processing and problem solving. The *Verbal IQ* subtests assess a student's verbal ability, general knowledge base, and language development skills. The *Performance IQ* subtests assess nonverbal reasoning and visual perceptual skills, as well as speed of information processing. Both the verbal and performance subtests combine to yield an overall or Full Scale score. *It should be cautioned that intelligence tests do not measure important attributes for learning such as creativity, motivation to learn, or personality styles, though they remain an excellent predictor of academic success.*

Richard's *Full Scale IQ* was in the *Average* range of functioning, and at the *32ⁿᵈ* percentile compared to peers. His *Verbal IQ* was in the *Average* range, and at the *30ᵗʰ* percentile, while his *Performance IQ* was in the *Average* range, and at the *39ᵗʰ* percentile compared to peers. *The difference between his verbal and nonverbal problem solving skills was not significant.* The rest of his domain scores were as follows:

| Verbal | SS | Performance | SS |
|---|---|---|---|
| Information | 9 | Picture Completion | 13 |
| Similarities | 10 | Coding | 7 |
| Arithmetic | 5 | Picture Arrangement | 12 |
| Vocabulary | 9 | Block Design | 6 |
| Comprehension | 10 | Object Assembly | 9 |
| Digit Span | 4 | | |

*Mean = 10*

**RANGE**

| | | |
|---|---|---|
| Verbal IQ | 92 (86 - 99) | AVERAGE |
| Performance IQ | 96 (88 - 104) | AVERAGE |
| Full Scale IQ | 93 (88 - 99) | AVERAGE |

Within the verbal domain, Richard demonstrated good language development and verbal comprehension skills. He had little difficulty defining individual vocabulary words, in addition to determining common relationships between pairs of words. Higher scores in these areas often suggest strong verbal concept development. His general knowledge of facts and events was sound. Richard responded well to questions pertaining to social rules and regulations, suggesting good expressive language skills. However, relative weaknesses were observed on tasks requiring short-term memory skills, and the ability to sustain a visual image in mind. For instance, he struggled when repeating back digits heard aloud, as well as when solving arithmetic problems in his head.

Richard's nonverbal problem solving skills were roughly equivalent to his overall verbal abilities. Relative strengths were noted in his ability to sequence *mixed up* pictures in order to tell a meaningful story, as well as when deciphering missing details in pictures. Stronger scores in these areas often suggest good logical problem solving skills, as well as good visual perception to detailed information. Richard had difficulty with more "higher level" visual/spatial skills, such as when arranging blocks to make various shapes. A mild weakness was also observed on a paper and pencil task requiring him to copy various symbols when timed. ***Richard's overall profile of scores indicated he had average general problem solving skills, with weaknesses noted on more visual/spatial types of tasks requiring him to generate a visual image in the mind's eye.***

**VISUAL/PERCEPTUAL TESTS:** On the *Bender-Gestalt,* a test of visual perceptual skills requiring students to copy nine geometric designs, Richard's scores suggested an age-equivalency of **8 years 6 months to 8 years 11 months.** This was in the **Low Average** range of functioning, as Richard had mild difficulty copying shapes that overlapped together. There were no significant distortions or rotations noted with his drawings, though he bunched most of them toward the top half of his paper.

The *Jordan Left-Right Reversal Test* assesses visual reversals of letters, numbers, and words in young children. Richard's responses indicated a developmental age score that was in the **Average** range, though he made one error in reversing a *"b"* for *"d"*. Nevertheless, this suggested little difficulty with visual perception of letters and numbers. It should be noted that most beginning readers tend to make frequent reversals, and often, students with poor attention to detail tend to struggle on this task.

**READING MEASURES:** The *Gray-Oral Reading Test* was administered in order to assess Richard's ability to read with speed and accuracy, in addition to evaluate his overall comprehension skills. His oral reading quotient was **52 +/-7,** which was in the

*Moderately Impaired* range, and less than the *1st* percentile compared to peers. This corresponded to a grade equivalency score of approximately a late *1st to beginning 2nd* grade level. Richard was a very slow and labored oral reader, and had a tendency to substitute whole words when reading. He relied heavily on his sight word recognition skills, and appeared to have few words that he could automatically recognize. This type of reading style, relying on the visual gestalt or contour of a word instead of using phonemic strategies, is typical among students with a learning disability. An error analysis indicated the following miscues:

| **SEMANTIC ERRORS** | **VISUAL ERRORS** |
|---|---|
| "stars" . . . . . ."stripes" | "having" . . . . ."hard" |
| "parents". . . ."people" | "for" . . . . . . ."from" |
| "boards" . . . ."bottles" | "his". . . . . . ."this" |
| "dirty" . . . . . ."dry" | "around" . . . ."along" |

**DEEP DYSLEXIA HYPOTHESIS:** Richard's particular error patterns were consistent with *deep dyslexia,* a type of *double deficit* reading disability characterized by poor phonemic awareness creating an over-reliance on visual cues to identify words. However, there appeared to be restricted access to certain families of words using solely visual cues. In essence, reading concrete, highly imaginable words (nouns such as *monkey, chair, table*) are easier to read since these words can be visualized quite clearly. Conversely, words that are more abstract in nature, and much more difficult to visualize (words such as *idea, peace, concept*) are more difficult to read. Since Richard relied so heavily on visual analysis and meaning to decipher words (instead of phonemic cues), his errors tended to be whole word substitutions of similar meaning, or of similar shape. Many errors were also seen among smaller words such as *"the", "is",* and *"was",* as Richard was unable to use decoding strategies, and often substituted unrelated words in their place.

The following neuropsychological measures were administered to confirm the hypothesis that Richard's reading difficulties were due to **deep dyslexia.** Once again, the expected deficit patterns would entail an inability to decode words using grapheme to phoneme (symbol/sound) correspondence, an over-reliance on visual gestalt or contours of words, predictable error patterns, and an inability to access certain classes of words.

**NEUROPSYCHOLOGICAL MEASURES:** Various subtests from the *NEPSY,* a developmental neuropsychological instrument, were administered in order to determine specific processing deficits that may be hindering Richard's ability to read.

Often, students with difficulty in reading and written language also tend to struggle on language related processing measures. For most right-handed students, these tasks include phonological awareness, rapidly naming items, and interpreting oral instructions. All are presumed to be mediated by left temporal lobe functioning. Conversely, students with difficulty in math, handwriting, or other paper and pencil tasks often have subtle, underlying visual spatial processing deficits, which may implicate either left or right parietal lobe functioning. Richard's scores were as follows:

| SUBTEST | SS = 10 | RANGE |
|---|---|---|
| Phonological Processing | 4 | Well Below Average |
| Speeded Naming | 7 | Low Average |
| Comprehension of Instructions | 9 | Average |
| Verbal Fluency: Semantic Items (Food/Drink) | 18 /min | Average |
| Verbal Fluency: Phonemic Items (S & F words) | 4 /min | Well Below Average |
| **\*Composite Language Score** | **70** | **Borderline** |

Richard's composite language score was **70,** which was only in the **Borderline** range of development, and at the **2nd** percentile compared to peers. His subtest scores indicated extremely limited phonemic awareness skills, as well as poorly developed categorization of words by phonemic properties. For instance, he had difficulty identifying words from segments (i.e. say the word *mistaken* without the *mis*), as well as creating new words by substituting sounds (i.e. say *hope* substituting "z" for "p"). A relative strength was noted in his ability to comprehend instructions with 3 and 4 step commands. However, he had extreme difficulty rapidly naming words based upon phonemic instead of semantic properties. For example, Richard was able to effectively name categories of animals or foods, but was unable to name items that started with the letter *"f"* or *"s"*.

**NEPSY SUMMARY:** *Richard clearly had difficulty with phonological processing skills, a task usually mediated by the left temporal lobe (superior temporal sulcus). Much research indicates that students who have not grasped sound/symbol correspondence by age 12 may never acquire this skill, and need to rely on generating visual images or "sight word" scanning to develop effective reading skills. Furthermore, Richard categorizes information based upon meaning (semantic clustering) and could not access language very effectively using phonemic (letter) cues.*

**MEMORY TESTS:** The *California Verbal Learning Test-Children's Version* was administered to assess the strategies Richard used when learning verbal information.

Richard was presented with a list of 15 words to recall under three conditions: *immediate recall, short-term recall with a distracter, and long-term recall 20 minutes later.* In the first trial, Richard was able to recall **7 of 15** words, which was well within the Average range. However, by the 5th trial, Richard was able to recall just **9 of 15** words which indicated a learning slope in the **Low Average** range. This suggested a slower paced learning curve when learning and retaining new information. Richard tended to recall only words toward the end of the list, and was not able to recall words from the middle of the list very efficiently. This suggested a very passive learning strategy when presented with new information. Richard did not cluster the items into semantic categories (i.e. *fruits, clothing,* etc.) very successfully, instead relying on the most recent words heard as his sole recalling cue.

Next, Richard was asked to recall another list of 15 words, of which he was able to recall **6 of 15.** When asked to then recall words from the initial list (List A which he had 5 trials to learn the words), he was able to recall just **7 of 15** words, the same score on his initial trial. This suggested a fairly rapid rate of forgetting, due in part to his tendency to recall words by serial position (most recent word heard) as opposed to utilizing other strategies. However, after a long delay, Richard was still able to recall **7 of 15** words on the original list.

The visual memory subtests only from the **Wide Range Assessment of Memory and Learning Test** was administered and Richard scored **95,** which was in the Average range and at the 37th percentile compared to peers. He performed best when recalling visual scenes and images that were highly meaningful, such as when asked to recall scenes from a beach or farm. Richard had increasingly more difficulty when asked to recall nonmeaningful visual information, such as repeating a rote sequence on the finger windows card.

**MEMORY SUMMARY:** *Richard had a rapid rate of forgetting verbal information due to insufficient memory strategies. He had a passive learning strategy, meaning he was able to recall the most recently heard information, and did not chunk words very efficiently into semantic categories. His visual memory skills were age-appropriate for highly meaningful and concrete images, though somewhat suspect for more abstract spatial sequences.*

**BEHAVIOR MEASURES:** The **Piers-Harris Self-Concept Scale** evaluates self-esteem across a variety of interpersonal domains. Richard's overall score was in the Average range of development, suggesting he would feel fairly self-assured in most

interpersonal situations. However, there were specific concerns regarding his overall academic confidence, especially with reading. For instance, Richard indicated he was extremely sensitive about his reading deficiencies, and tended to become quite anxious when asked to read in class. He mentioned he was poor in his schoolwork, and felt that his parents expected too much from him. At times, he may act in a defiant manner rather than risk the embarrassment of reading in front of others.

**SUMMARY AND RECOMMENDATIONS:** Richard is a 12 year-old student currently in the 6th grade at White Oak Middle School. He was referred for a complete dyslexia evaluation due to continued difficulty acquiring and retaining basic reading skills. According to his special education teacher, Richard's reading skills tended to plateau around a 2nd grade level, and he continues to make semantic substitutions when reading, as well as have difficulty decoding smaller words. Current testing revealed his overall cognitive abilities were in the ***Average*** range of functioning ***(FSIQ = 93)*** with his verbal and nonverbal problem solving skills being roughly equivalent. ***Richard's overall profile of scores indicated he had average general problem solving skills, with weaknesses noted on more visual/spatial types of tasks requiring him to generate a visual image in the mind's eye.***

Further testing indicated his overall reading skills were significantly impaired, and on approximately a ***beginning 2nd*** grade level. An analysis of his reading skills suggested his error patterns were consistent with ***deep dyslexia,*** a type of reading disability characterized by poor phonemic awareness creating an over-reliance on visual cues to identify words. Unfortunately, the only strategy that Richard used to unlock the reading code was to rely on *meaning* to conjure up a visual image of the target word. In essence, reading concrete, highly imaginable words (nouns such as *monkey, chair, table*) were easier to read since these words can be visualized quite clearly. Conversely, words that were more abstract in nature, and much more difficult to visualize (words such as *idea, peace, concept*) were more difficult to read. This hypothesis seemed to account for Richard's peculiar pattern of semantic substitutions. Further memory testing suggested his visual memory skills were age-appropriate for highly meaningful and concrete images (as predicted), though somewhat suspect for more abstract spatial sequences.

Lastly, Richard also had a tendency to decipher words more effectively when spelled aloud instead of identifying them in print. Perhaps in some instances, he used an acoustic strategy to help decode certain words that he otherwise would have no access using just a whole word approach. In other words, his processing style may restrict his access to certain words stored in the left hemisphere, unless presented in an auditory fashion.

Once again, hearing words accesses different neural pathways than seeing words. Given this scenario, the following recommendations are offered:

1. The IEP Committee needs to convene in order to determine the appropriateness of an alpha-phonics model of reading given Richard's specific type of reading disability. Results from this evaluation need to be compared with information gathered from the multi-disciplinary team before a final decision can be made.

2. Treatment of **deep dyslexia** is often difficult given the *double deficit* nature of the disorder. Research has shown that the key lies in fooling the brain into a phonemic classification system. However, the phonemes need to be highly concrete, easily visualized words, not sounds. For instance, the following procedures may be useful:

   a)  Have Richard take each letter of the alphabet and **link** it with a highly visual word of his choice. For instance "M" could be linked with "money". Mnemonic strategies may be needed to develop a link for each letter of the alphabet.
   b)  Next, segment off the word to just its initial phoneme sound (e.g. M=m).
   c)  Sound out each letter for monosyllabic words.
   d)  Based upon an error analysis of misread words, teach Richard to use a phonemic approach to words he cannot decode by meaning.

3. Build word recognition skills using a word bank and color coding method. In other words, based upon Edward Fry's list of the 1000 most recognizable words, have Richard learn these words in context and color code different parts of speech. Once learned, have him recognize these words out of context, though color coded as his cue for recognition. Finally, present the words without the color coding.

4. Richard's overall written language skills need to be improved. Have him keep a journal or diary each day to practice writing skills. Also, he may benefit from learning how to use a computer for longer writing assignments.

5. Richard may benefit from taking tests and quizzes in his special education classroom to help eliminate distractions. This may also alleviate some of his anxiety toward reading in front of others.

6. Richard's teachers should not ask him to read aloud in front of others, as this only heightens his anxiety level toward reading and leads to increased frustration.

# DIANE

***Case #2:*** Diane was referred for a dyslexia evaluation due to continued difficulty developing her overall reading skills. Assessment was administered in order to determine her future educational needs.

## TESTS ADMINISTERED:
Wechsler Intelligence Scale for Children-Third Edition (WISC-III)
Developmental Test of Visual-Motor Integration (VMI)
Jordan Left-Right Reversal Test
NEPSY (selected subtests)
California Verbal Learning Test-Children's Version
Informal Writing Sample
Attention Deficit Disorder's Evaluation Scale: School Version

**BACKGROUND INFORMATION:** Diane is a 6 year-old student currently in the 1st grade at White Oak Elementary School. She was referred for a complete evaluation due to continued difficulty developing her overall reading skills. According to her 1st grade teacher, Diane's classroom performance has been somewhat inconsistent, and she has made little progress with her reading and language arts skills. Her teacher indicated that Diane's overall reading skills were on approximately a pre-primer level, while her math skills were on a 1st grade level. Diane was also described as having difficulty with spelling and written language skills, and there were noted concerns regarding her attention and concentration as well. For instance, her teacher mentioned that Diane had difficulty initiating new tasks, was easily distracted, and struggled to work independently in class. There were no behavior concerns reported by the school, and Diane's daily attendance has been satisfactory. She currently receives speech and language services, due to noticeable articulation errors.

**DEVELOPMENTAL HISTORY:** Currently, Diane lives at home with her mother, an older brother, and her grandparents. There were no specific prenatal concerns reported by her mother, and Diane weighed 8 pounds 2 ounces at birth. Most developmental milestones were reported as being reached within normal limits, with the exception of speech acquisition skills. Diane attended Head Start for approximately 2 years prior to entering kindergarten. There was no history of learning difficulty on her mother's side, though it was reported that Diane's biological father had difficulty in school, and received both speech and language therapy services as well as special education services for a language based learning disability. Diane's parents were never married, and she has

infrequent contact with her biological father. Diane indicated she enjoyed school and perceived herself to be a good student.

**TEST RESULTS AND INTERPRETATIONS:** Diane was administered the *WISC-III* in order to assess her overall level of cognitive functioning. *It should be cautioned that intelligence tests at this age merely reflect the rate of cognitive development, and do not necessarily predict future academic success. Further, they do not measure important attributes for learning such as creativity, motivation to learn, or personality styles.*

Diane's *Full Scale IQ* was in the *Average* range of functioning, and at the **39**th percentile compared to peers. Her *Verbal IQ* was in the lower end of the *Average* range, and at the **25**th percentile, while her *Performance IQ* was in the *Average* range, and at the **61**st percentile compared to peers. *The difference between her verbal and nonverbal problem solving skills was statistically significant.* The rest of her domain scores were as follows:

| Verbal | SS | | Performance | SS |
|---|---|---|---|---|
| Information | 10 | | Picture Completion | 10 |
| Similarities | 6 | | Coding | 17 |
| Arithmetic | 5 | | Picture Arrangement | 9 |
| Vocabulary | 7 | | Block Design | 10 |
| Comprehension | 13 | | Object Assembly | 7 |
| Digit Span | 5 | | | |

*(Mean = 10)*

|  | | RANGE |
|---|---|---|
| Verbal IQ | 90 (84 - 97) | AVERAGE |
| Performance IQ | 104 (96 - 112) | AVERAGE |
| Full Scale IQ | 96 (91 - 102) | AVERAGE |

Within the verbal domain, Diane demonstrated below average language development and verbal comprehension skills. A relative strength was noted when responding to questions pertaining to practical knowledge and social rules (Comprehension). However, Diane had difficulty defining individual vocabulary words, and when determining common relationships between pairs of words. Lower scores in these areas often suggest weaker verbal concept development, and a limited general vocabulary base. Her general knowledge of facts and events was sound. Diane also had difficulty when solving orally presented math problems, suggesting poor "mental math" skills, as

well as inconsistent attention and concentration to the task at hand. A relative weakness was also observed in her ability to repeat back digits heard aloud, suggesting slightly below average short-term memory skills.

Diane's nonverbal problem solving skills were somewhat better developed than her overall verbal abilities, and there was more subtest scatter observed. A significant strength was noted when copying various shapes on a timed subtest (Coding). Stronger scores on this measure often indicate good visual-motor speed, and strong fine motor skill development. Diane performed adequately when arranging blocks and puzzles to form various designs, suggesting good visual/spatial and logical problem solving skills. Her overall visual perception to detailed information was sound. Lastly, she performed adequately when arranging "mixed up" pictures in a logical order to tell a meaningful story (Picture Arrangement), indicating good knowledge of cause and effect relationships. *Diane's overall profile of scores suggested she was more visual in her approach to learning, with weaknesses noted on tasks involving auditory short-term memory skills.*

**VISUAL/PERCEPTUAL TESTS:** On the *VMI,* a test of visual perceptual skills requiring students to copy various geometric designs, Diane scored *105,* which was in the *Average* range of functioning, and at the *63rd* percentile compared to peers. This score indicated little difficulty with visual-motor integration skills. Diane was right-handed and demonstrated an adequate pencil grip. Often, students with difficulty in visual-motor integration tend to struggle on most paper and pencil tasks, copying information from the board, and may have difficulty in math.

The *Jordan Left-Right Reversal Test* assesses visual reversals of letters, numbers, and words in young children. Diane's responses indicated a developmental age score that was *within normal limits.* Diane was easily able to recognize all of the letters on the page, and had little difficulty determining which letters and numbers were written backwards. It should be noted that most beginning readers tend to make frequent reversals, and often, students with learning disabilities or poor attention to detail tend to struggle on this task.

**NEUROPSYCHOLOGICAL MEASURES:** Various subtests from the *NEPSY,* a developmental neuropsychological instrument, were administered in order to determine specific processing deficits that may be hindering Diane's ability to read. Often, students with difficulty in reading and written language also tend to struggle on language related processing measures. For most students, these tasks include

phonological awareness, rapidly naming items, and interpreting oral instructions. All are presumed to be mediated by left temporal lobe functioning, the same region which plays a vital role in acquiring basic reading skills. Diane's scores were as follows:

| SUBTEST | SS = 10 | RANGE |
|---|---|---|
| Phonological Processing | 7 | Low Average |
| Speeded Naming | 1 | Impaired |
| Comprehension of Instructions | 6 | Low Average |
| Verbal Fluency: Animal Naming | 10 /min | Average |
| Verbal Fluency: Food/Drink Naming | 6 /min | Average |
| *Composite Language Score | 64 | Impaired |

Diane's composite language score was **64,** which was in the **Impaired** range of development, and only at the **1**st percentile compared to peers. This score suggested Diane lacked many prerequisite skills in order for adequate reading development to commence. For instance, she had difficulty identifying words from segments (i.e. say the word *"inside"* without the *"in"*) suggesting poor phonological awareness, and she was unable to rapidly name objects in an accurate manner. Lower scores in these areas are usually an accurate predictor of future reading difficulty. In addition, Diane had difficulty comprehending 2-3 step verbal instructions suggesting poor auditory attention and short-term memory skills. Diane performed better when rapidly naming objects from specific semantic categories (animals, foods, etc.), suggesting that access to information in her lexicon was most easily retrieved using semantic cues.

**MEMORY TESTS:** The *California Verbal Learning Test-Children's Version* was administered to assess the strategies and processes Diane used when learning verbal information. She was presented with a list of 15 words to recall under *three conditions: immediate recall, short-term recall with a distracter, and long-term recall of the list 20 minutes later.* In the first condition (List A), Diane was only able to recall *3 of 15* words in the first trial, which suggested a poor active working memory and weak auditory attention span. By the 5th trial, Diane was now able to recall *7 of 15* words which indicated a below average learning slope across each trial. In other words, after 5 trials of learning List A, she was now able to learn *four* additional words. This suggested a below average learning curve and difficulty with verbal short-term memory skills. Diane tended to recall few words from the beginning of the list, though was able to use appropriate learning strategies, as she chunked items by their semantic category (fruits, clothing, etc.) when recalling them.

Next, Diane was asked to recall another list of 15 words (List B), which again, she was able to recall just **3 of 15.** Once again, this score indicated poor auditory attention skills. When asked to recall List A (for the 6th time) immediately following the initial presentation of List B, she was only able to recall **5 of 15** items. This suggested that Diane seemed to be prone to forgetting information when distracted, and could reflect an inability to store information in an efficient manner while in short-term memory. Lastly, following a 20-minute delay, Diane was able to recall **5 of 15** words from List A, indicating an average rate of retention. *In sum, Diane appeared to have limited auditory short-term memory skills, and may be prone to forgetting information in short-term memory when distracted.*

**INFORMAL WRITING SAMPLE:** An informal writing sample was obtained by having Diane write down three wishes. She was unable to adequately construct a sentence, and rarely capitalized the first word of each sentence, or put periods at the end of sentences. The content of her sentences was somewhat limited, and consisted mainly of two or three word phrases. She had difficulty with spelling, and her attempts were not always phonetically correct. In sum, Diane's writing sample appeared well below grade level.

**ATTENTION CHECKLISTS:** The *Attention Deficit Disorders Evaluation Scale* was completed by Diane's 1st grade teacher. This scale documents and describes three main characteristics associated with ADHD: namely, inattentiveness, hyperactivity, and impulse control difficulty. Diane was rated by her teacher as exhibiting these characteristics more frequently than **83 percent** of her peers. This was considered a **mildly significant** score. Diane was described as being somewhat disorganized in class, being easily distracted, having difficulty following verbal directions, and being easily upset. Still, there were few responses that indicated Diane had difficulty controlling her impulses, or was hyperactive in her manner.

**SUMMARY AND RECOMMENDATIONS:** Diane is a 6 year-old student currently in the 1st grade at White Oak Elementary School. She was referred for a complete evaluation due to continued difficulty developing her overall reading skills. According to her 1st grade teacher, Diane's classroom performance has been somewhat inconsistent, and there were noted concerns regarding her ability to focus her attention as well. Current testing revealed her overall cognitive abilities were in the *Average* range of functioning *(FSIQ = 96),* with her nonverbal skills being somewhat better developed than her verbal abilities. *Diane's overall profile of scores suggested she was more visual in her approach to learning, with weaknesses noted on tasks involving auditory short-term memory skills.*

Further testing indicated specific processing deficits that may be hindering her academic development in reading. Diane had difficulty with most phonemic awareness tasks, and was unable to rapidly name objects in an accurate manner. Lower scores in these areas are usually an accurate predictor of future reading difficulty. She performed much better when naming items from semantic categories (i.e. *animals, foods,* etc.) and on visual-motor types of tasks, suggesting an over-reliance on semantic and visual cues to decipher meaning from print, and an under-reliance on phonological and auditory cues. There were mild attentional concerns noted in the classroom as well, specifically during discussions and when listening to auditory directions. In summary, Diane presented the profile of a student with difficulty processing language in a rapid fashion, and lacked the phonological substructure for adequate reading skills to commence. Consequently, her attention tends to drift during listening tasks, and she has difficulty in keeping pace with the 1st grade curriculum. The following recommendations were offered:

1. Diane might benefit from an Orton-Gillingham based reading methodology in order to increase her phonological awareness skills. For instance, the alphabetic phonics program uses multi-sensory activities to teach coding patterns and letter sequences in order to learn individual sounds, syllables, and words.

2. Classroom modifications such as preferential seating close to the teacher, providing her with visual cues to accompany auditory directions, and using subtle re-focusing techniques such as a light tap of the shoulder may help her focus her attention better in class.

3. Diane's speech teacher may want to consider the Fast ForWord computer program, developed by Paula Tallal, which helps children with auditory perceptual deficits discriminate between rapidly presented sounds.

4. Diane's mother should read stories to her each night, as well as have her read at home to further enhance her reading skills.

5. Diane should keep a journal or diary at home to further practice her written language skills.

<big>The Timing of</big>
<big>Learning</big>

# Chapter 10

The language of the brain is encoded in neurons arranged in an astonishingly complex array of patterns and circuitry ever changing to the subtle deviations from our every day experiences. The education of the mind, or what is commonly referred to as learning, involves altering the brain's neural circuitry by linking new knowledges and experiences with previously stored information. Given the brain's 100 trillion or so connections among its 100 billion neurons, there is a seemingly infinite capacity for learning to take place. However, the rhythmic firing of neurons does not happen automatically, but rather requires enriched experiences and stimulation during certain critical periods in the life cycle of a brain cell. For instance, children whose mothers talk to them more frequently stimulate the language centers of the brain, and will develop better verbal skills (Kotulak, 1997). In other words, mental stimulation during early childhood activates brain cells to organize synaptic connections into networks for processing new information and setting down memories. It is during this critical period, and especially the first three years of life, that the foundations for thinking, language, vision, attitudes, aptitudes, and a host of other characteristics are laid down in the basic wiring of our brains. Then the windows in the brain close, and much of the fundamental architecture is completed (Kotulak, 1997).

Take for example the acquisition of language. Every child is born with the ability to discriminate all sounds. However, based upon exposure to cultural dialects, a child becomes tuned only to sounds from the host language. The concept of *pruning* refers to the brain's ability to discard cells that seemingly have no particular function.

Therefore, if cells designated to decipher a particular sound were never exposed to that sound, these cells either die or reorganize to assume another function. Our sound categories are formed by experience as infants become attuned to the peculiarities of their host language. In the process, a baby loses the ability to detect subtle differences in speech sounds once earlier perceived. Therefore, permanent mental models of sound categories are formed and slight variations become ignored. This is why children born in another country continue to have foreign accents if brought to the United States past age five, but speak fluently if exposed to English prior to age five when permanent sound categories have not yet been established. The brain seems to be the ultimate *use it* or *lose it* type of organ. Consequently, the *timing* of learning and exposure to sensory stimuli becomes as crucial an element as the quality of the learning experience itself.

Perhaps no other neurological concept has had as profound of an effect on teachers and parents than the knowledge that sensory experience is essential for teaching brain cells their jobs, and after a certain critical period, brain cells lose the opportunity to perform these jobs (Ramachandran, 1998). For instance, if the brain does not process visual experiences by age two, the capacity will be lost, and if a child is never exposed to language by age 10, the person will never acquire this skill (Kotulak, 1997). Therefore, the key to educating the brain lies in the ability to stimulate and enrich certain brain regions at critical junctures in the developing nervous system.

Neuroscientists have demonstrated there is a natural sequencing or unfolding of cell behavior, pre-programmed by millions of years of evolution, which follows a predictable developmental course from conception through childhood. During gestation, the brain grows at an incredible rate of several hundred thousand cells per minute (Chase, 1996). As brain cells proliferate and divide in the developing fetus, they migrate to their designated locations and begin to establish basic neural connections. By day 45, the cerebral hemispheres have already formed, and by week 24, the traditional layering of the cerebral cortex is found (Kolb & Whishaw, 1996). At birth, a baby's brain contains as many cells as stars in the Milky Way galaxy, approximately 100 billion, and this overproduction of brain cells seems to be evolution's way of ensuring the development of the many new skills which await. During the first 2 or 3 years postnatally, neurons form an overabundance of synapses, or connections between cells, and often brain damage during this period allows for a certain plasticity of functions, as the brain can more easily reorganize itself. ***Pruning*** is an evolutionary necessity and involves a reduction of dendritic connections to develop maximum efficiency of a particular skill. Once a neural network has been established, support cells begin to surround the network of axons and the ***myelination*** process begins (Kolb & Whishaw, 1996). The

myelination of various brain regions begins in infancy and continues into adulthood, and signals the full maturity and *hard wiring* of certain brain regions. Hence, there are certain windows of opportunity for learning based upon the developing nervous system, brain growth spurts, and subsequent myelination process. Table 10-1 summarizes the most opportune time for learning:

TABLE 10-1

| THE TIMING OF LEARNING | | |
|---|---|---|
| **AGE** | **SKILL** | **BRAIN REGION** |
| 3 -10 months | Attention & Awareness | Reticular Formation |
| 2 - 4 years | Language Acquisition | Temporal Lobes |
| 6 - 8 years | Phonemic Development | Inferior Parietal and Temporal Lobes |
| 10 - 12 years | Abstract Language | Inferior Parietal Lobes and Frontal Lobes |
| 14 - 16 years | Judgement & Planning | Frontal Lobes |

*Increment in brain weight 5-10 percent over each 2 year period
*Expansion not due to neuronal proliferation, but rather growth in dendritic processes and myelination.

The most essential remediation strategy of dyslexia lies not in a particular reading program, series, or educational methodology, but rather lies in the *timing* of when to introduce a particular reading program, series, or educational strategy based upon an individual learner's neurodevelopmental profile. As mentioned previously, much research has shown that children who have not developed phonological awareness by age 9 or 10 probably have lost the capacity to do so (Rourke, 1994). Once again, cells that are responsible for processing sounds in a symbolic fashion will decline when not used, and eventually die out (pruning) or find another functional means to gravitate towards (Kotulak, 1997). Nevertheless, there are many educators who insist that phonological awareness is the only viable methodology to instill reading success in students, even when in high school. Despite years of dwindling results, educators cling to the *magic bullet* theory of finding the right reading program, yet ignore the neurodevelopmental sequelae that enables successful learning to occur. Table 10-2 outlines the developmental progression of normal language and motor skill development so there is a basic understanding of the neurodevelopmental needs of the learner.

## TABLE 10-2

**DEVELOPMENTAL MILESTONES IN MOTOR AND LANGUAGE DEVELOPMENT**

(Kolb & Fantie, in press)

| At the completion of: | Vocalization and Language |
|---|---|
| 12 weeks | Markedly less crying than at 8 weeks; when talked to and nodded at, smiles, followed by squealing-gurgling sounds usually called cooing, which is vowel-like in character and pitch-modulated; sustains cooing for 15-20 seconds. |
| 16 weeks | Responds to human sounds more definitely; turns head; eyes seem to search for speaker; occasionally some chuckling sounds. |
| 20 weeks | The vowel-like cooing sounds begin to be interspersed with more consonantal sounds; labial fricatives, spirants, and nasals are common; acoustically, all vocalizations are very different from the sounds of the mature language of the environment. |
| 6 months | Cooing changing into babbling resembling one-syllable utterances; neither vowels nor consonants have very fixed recurrences; most common utterances sound somewhat like ma, mu, da, or di. |
| 8 months | Reduplication (or more continuous repetitions) becomes frequent; intonation patterns become distinct; utterances can signal emphasis and emotions. |
| 10 months | Vocalizations are mixed with sound-play such as gurgling or bubble-blowing; appears to wish to imitate sounds, but the limitations are never quite successful; beginning to differentiate between words heard by making differential adjustment. |
| 12 months | Identical sound sequences are replicated with higher relative frequency of occurrence and words (mamma or dadda) are emerging; definite signs of understanding some words and simple commands (show me your eyes) |
| 18 months | Has a definite repertoire of words-more than 3 but less than 50; still much babbling but now of several syllables with intricate intonation pattern; no attempt at communicating information and no frustration for not being understood; words may include items such as thank you or come here, but there is little ability to join any of the lexical items into spontaneous two-item phrases; understanding is progressing rapidly. |
| 24 months | Vocabulary of more than 50 items (some children seem to be able to name everything in the environment); begins spontaneously to join vocabulary items into two-word phrases; all phrases appear to be own creations; increase in communicative behavior and interest in language |
| 30 months | Fastest increase in vocabulary with many new additions every day; no babbling at all; utterances have communicative intent; frustrated if not understood by adults; utterances consist of at least two words, many have three or even five words; sentences and phrases have characteristic child grammar, that is, they are rarely verbatim repetitions of an adult utterance; intelligibility is not very good yet, though there is great variation among children; seems to understand everything that is said to him. |
| 3 years | Vocabulary of some 1000 words; about 80% of utterances are intelligible even to strangers; grammatical complexity of utterances is roughly that of colloquial adult language, although mistakes still occur |
| 4 years | Language is well established; deviations from the adult norm tend to be more in style than in grammar |

# remediation techniques

# Chapter 11

There are literally thousands of reading programs used by professional educators today, each of which has its merits as well as flaws. Professional educators often become enamored with a particular reading series, then over time become disenchanted with the results, and quickly switch their allegiance to the next *magic bullet* approach to reading. The rationale for presenting a few of the more popular approaches to reading is to highlight some of the diversity between programs, as well as point out how each plays a vital role in strengthening the neurological integrity of the neural circuitry in reading. The following reading programs will be discussed from the standpoint of timing, more than content, so there is a basic understanding of when to match a particular reading program with the neurodevelopmental needs of the learner. As Hynd (1986) points out, there are four key steps in determining which program has the greatest chance for success with an individual student:

## TABLE 11-1

| STEPS IN CHOOSING AN EFFECTIVE INTERVENTION |
|---|

1) Determine a profile of strengths and weaknesses. Then try to classify the child into a particular subtype of dyslexia based upon their error analysis.
2) Infer neurological processing which is required for normal reading based upon the age and education level of the child.
3) Determine at what point the child's processing breaks down and the subsequent compensation strategies the child uses.
4) Find instructional strategies that match a student's specific learning style.

## STRATEGIES FOR YOUNGER STUDENTS:

Perhaps the most efficient strategy to ensure a normal developmental progression for reading lies in the architecture of language. Enriching the linguistic foundation in preschool children, when the brain is most apt to acquire word knowledge, provides children with an opportunity to develop naming skills, rapid retrieval skills, and other linguistic capabilities that stimulate the neural pathways for subsequent reading to occur. Therefore, the first strategy toward remediating dyslexia lies with parents, as opposed to a specific academic program, to consistently expose children to verbal cues in their environment as well as to introduce literacy as a pleasurable activity. For instance, the average number of words spoken in a professional home daily is approximately 1,500 to 2,500, which equates to a child hearing about 35 million spoken words by age three. Conversely, the number of words spoken in a middle class home is between 1,000 to 1,500, which equates to a child hearing about 20 million words spoken by age three. Lastly, the number of words spoken by mothers on welfare is approximately 500 to 800 words, which equates to just 10 million words heard by age three (Hart & Risley, 1995). Notwithstanding, the following programs are recommended to enhance the reading skills in younger children, regardless of the linguistic foundation provided for at home.

***FAST ForWord:*** A computer program designed to help children distinguish among phonemes, first at artificially slowed rates of speech, then at normal rates. Much of the conceptual underpinnings stem from the research of Tallal et. al. (1993). It was found that many reading disabled children suffered from auditory perceptual deficits that interfered with their ability to identify rapidly changing acoustical elements embedded in speech. Reading difficulties were assumed to be caused by the brain's inability to rapidly process

consonant sounds, which are spoken at a much faster rate than vowel sounds. Consequently, it was very difficult to distinguish a *"ba"* sound from a *"da"* sound. This condition presumably interfered with the reading process, since children cannot match sounds they cannot hear. Her research showed that normal children take just ten milliseconds to distinguish between these sounds, but reading disabled children require hundreds of milliseconds. Therefore, Tallal et. al. (1993) predicted that reading impairments associated with phonological discrimination were caused by slow auditory perceptual processing, and phonological deficits should improve when listening to these sounds synthetically prolonged via a computer format.

*Instruction:* The training is fairly intense, as students must sit before computers for 100 minutes a day, five days a week, for approximately eight weeks. Two words, whose sounds differ only by their first letters, appear on the screen. The child must select the word, by clicking on a mouse, heard through headphones. There are various other activities, but most involve clicking on the screen based upon sounds heard through the headphones. The goals is to incrementally become faster and faster on this skill. A successful training program allows reading disabled children to distinguish among speech sounds as rapidly as *normal* children.

*Clinical Utility: Fast ForWord* and other similar types of computerized software programs tend to help children with central auditory processing deficits by allowing them to more clearly distinguish among sounds. However, this does not always translate into becoming a more effective reader. Nevertheless, for young children between the ages of 5 and 10, when the brain is at a critical juncture for phoneme classification, this program may prove very useful toward strengthening temporal lobe sensitivity for dysphonetic readers. Once again, this program may help with phonics knowledge; namely the lower level pairing of sounds with symbols, but not necessarily with phonics awareness, which involve higher level metacognitive skills that involve the sequential arrangement of sounds into words. From a neuropsychological perspective, much emphasis is based upon strengthening the role of the superior temporal gyrus.

*EAROBICS:* A computer program published by Cognitive Concepts designed to develop effective listening comprehension skills, phonological awareness, and auditory processing skills. Six activities are each automatically adjusted to a level of difficulty based upon the child's performance. These activities involve sequencing sounds, naming and identifying sounds, rhyming activities, discriminating among different sounds, and combining sound segments. *Earobics I,* which is designed for children ages 4 to 7, is an entertaining method to enhance auditory processing skills among young children. The

program has been translated into eight languages, and has been popular among speech therapists, ESL teachers, and reading specialists. **Earobics II** is similar in that the focus is to teach children auditory processing and phonemic awareness skills, though the program is targeted for children ages 7 to 10. There is more emphasis on isolating sounds, word closure, phoneme and syllable synthesis, and language comprehension as well. Once again, this is an adaptive training program in that levels automatically increase or decrease according to the child's performance.

**Instruction:** Recommended use is 15 minutes per day at least three times a week to show significant gains. As with most computerized programs, most students need minimal, if any assistance from an instructor. At sign-in, the child can select from one of three difficulty levels, and visual feedback is given for each activity completed successfully. Most activities are timed, and numerous animated features reward children for successful responses. The cost of the program remains relatively inexpensive for home use ($59.00).

**Clinical Utility:** The theoretical concept behind *Earobics* is the notion that phonological awareness is the fundamental code necessary for future reading skills to commence. This program offers promising results in that it circumvents many pitfalls normally associated with many phonemic-based interventions for reading. According to McGuinness (1997), most phonetically based reading programs fail for one of the following reasons:

TABLE 11-2

**REASONS PHONICS PROGRAMS TEND TO FAIL**

1. Loses a child's attention
2. Fails to teach all 44 phonemes
3. Fails to teach phoneme manipulation, segmenting, and blending
4. Programs are visually driven and not phonemically driven
5. Too many rules to memorize
6. Teaches reading and spelling as two separate processes instead of one reversible process based on the alphabetic code
7. Organizes by letter patterns and not phoneme patterns
8. Clusters the wrong perceptual units; for instance, consonant clusters and word families should be taught as one sound (i.e., wrist, rist)

From a neuropsychological perspective, *Earobics* places much emphasis upon strengthening the role of the superior temporal gyrus to enhance proper auditory discrimination of sounds. However, the program also works to strengthen other facets of the articulatory loop, particularly the role of the angular gyrus in phoneme manipulation and the sequential arrangement of sounds to words. Therefore, unlike the *Fast ForWord* program, both phonics knowledge and phonics awareness are emphasized.

**PHONO-GRAPHIX:** *Phono-Graphix* is a reading methodology developed by Read America and researched extensively by the University of South Florida. It bills itself as being a *pure* reading method, though in actuality it is an explicit phonics instruction program adhering rigidly to only those skills critical for reading. These skills involve auditory processing, which is the ability to segment, blend, and manipulate sounds in words, as well as specific training in the alphabetic code. *Phono-Graphix* addresses a fundamental pitfall with most phonics-based programs in that the written language code is not taught backwards. In other words, the emphasis is on teaching sounds to symbols, or what is referred to as sound pictures, instead of teaching symbols to sounds. Each activity teaches children to integrate motor, visual, and auditory cues as they read and spell, again emphasizing a multisensory approach to reading. There is also training in using appropriate versus inappropriate cognitive strategies when reading.

**Clinical Utility:** The authors claim that *Phono-Graphix* has shown to be 98% effective in helping all readers, even those with disabilities. For example, scores on the word attack and word identification section of the Woodcock-Johnson Test of Achievement have risen by one grade level in an average of 12 hours of one-on-one training. Advantage Learning Services offers both instruction and training for teachers in this reading methodology. From a neuropsychological perspective, this program seems narrow in scope, though may be useful for a child with an emerging dysphonetic dyslexia. Little emphasis is given toward reading comprehension or reading fluency and speed. However, much emphasis is placed toward automatizing the sound/symbol code in the English language, a skill seemingly subserved by the insular cortex in skilled readers.

## STRATEGIES FOR ELEMENTARY STUDENTS:

As previously mentioned, a plethora of reading programs exist for elementary-age students, though many seem to lack the necessary scope and comprehensiveness for meaningful gains among students with disabilities. In fact, the majority of reading programs were not necessarily designed for children in need of specialized instruction, but rather attempt to justify their proficiency by improving the skills for already competent readers. As McGuinness (1997) points out, there are certain prerequisites necessary for effective reading instructional programs.

### TABLE 11-3

**PRIMARY COMPONENTS OF AN EFFECTIVE BEGINNING READING PROGRAM**

1. <u>Phoneme Awareness</u> - training in awareness of phonemes in speech and the ability to segment and blend isolated phonemes
2. <u>Alphabetic Principle</u> - teaching the alphabetic code from sound to print
3. <u>Sound to Symbol Association</u> - teaching how to connect phonemes in words to individual letters and letter combinations
4. <u>Logic</u> - sequencing instruction in a logical order from simple to complex and conforming to a child's developmental level; should include the entire spelling code and not just a fraction of it
5. <u>Curriculum</u> - covering all possible skill areas including phoneme analysis, segmenting, blending, reading, writing, and spelling
6. <u>Pedagogic Style</u> - teaching by exposure and example using brief and clear explanations; ensuring that the child is actively problem-solving and not passive
7. <u>Fail Safe</u> - monitoring performance at frequent intervals

---

**ALPHABETIC PHONICS:** An expansion of the *Orton-Gillingham* multisensory approach for teaching reading to children with dyslexia. This program has been revised numerous times since its inception in the mid-1960s. The program assumes that 80 percent of the 30,000 most commonly used English words can be considered phonetically regular and therefore predictable once the basic rules have been learned (Clark & Uhry, 1995). Based upon Samuel Orton's theories, this program uses visual, auditory, and kinesthetic activities to develop a coding pattern for the English language. Progress is documented through benchmark measures, examining letter knowledge, alphabetizing skills, reading, spelling, and handwriting. The structured daily lesson takes an hour to complete, with 11

different activities lasting approximately 5 minutes each. This is an explicit (synthetic) type of phonics approach, as letter sound correspondences are taught in a *bottom-up* fashion before whole words are introduced. The program is designed for children from elementary school through high school, and there are numerous alpha-phonics teacher training centers throughout the United States.

***Clinical Utility:*** Despite the widespread inclusion of multisensory techniques in remedial programs for students with dyslexia, and the almost unanimous conviction among practitioners that they work, there is little empirical data to validate their effectiveness (Clark & Uhry, 1995). If anything, multisensory techniques appear to vary instructional activities and minimize boredom. An analysis of the human memory system explains why. Information stored in multiple areas of the brain can aid memory and be accessed more efficiently; however, the information is stored in a semantic manner. For instance, if learning the letter *"b"* by touch, this information is housed in the parietal lobes, by sight in the occipital/temporal lobes, and by sound in the temporal lobes. These are wonderful back-up strategies, but ultimately the letter *"b"* must be recognized by sight and encoded phonetically for reading to occur. Semantic memories, which are comprised of learned facts, are registered in the temporal lobes and retrieved by the frontal lobes (Carter, 1998). Therefore, multi-sensory techniques help with storage, though not necessarily with retrieval since only one sense, vision, is used to access information when reading. In other words, a good memory technique does not necessarily equate with an effective strategy for reading.

Notwithstanding, the *Alphabetic Phonics* program is one of the few reading programs proven successful with learning disabled children (Hutcheson et al., 1990). In particular, students with dysphonetic dyslexia would benefit most from this approach, as there is particular emphasis on developing the grapheme/phoneme code and using phonological cues to decipher meaning from print. There are many variations of the alphabetic phonics program, and the program is flexible enough to focus on emerging reading skills for elementary students, to more advance stages of reading comprehension and written language skills for secondary students. From a neuropsychological standpoint, much emphasis is spent on strengthening the phonological loop of reading that comprises the orthographic representation of sounds from the superior temporal gyrus, to the temporal order of sounds and syllables to words in the angular gyrus, to the production of sounds in Broca's area.

***Related Approaches:*** The ***Slingerland*** approach was designed by Beth Slingerland as an offshoot of the *Orton-Gillingham* approach to be used with whole classes. It relies

heavily on a multi-sensory format and was designed primarily for lower grades, though it can be adapted for use in the upper grades. A ***Visual-Auditory-Kinesthetic-Tactile (VAKT)*** approach to teach letters and sounds is used to lead toward automatic recall. There is nothing new about using a multi-sensory format, as these techniques date back to the 1920s, and were based on Samuel Orton's incorrect theory that dyslexia stems from incomplete cerebral dominance (Clark & Uhry, 1995). Unfortunately, modality specific instruction, which was extremely popular in the 1960s and 1970s, failed to take into account that regardless of the mode of input, words must eventually be recognized in a linguistic format based upon the neural circuitry of reading.

**READING RECOVERY:** *Reading Recovery* was developed in New Zealand in the mid-1970s and primarily focuses on low achieving 1ˢᵗ grade children. It is a one-on-one reading program typically lasting 30 minutes a day for each student. The length of the program varies from 12 to 20 weeks. *Reading Recovery* views reading as the act of constructing meaning. Each half hour is constructed around seven activities: 1) re-reading familiar books, 2) re-reading books with a running record of observed strategies and error analysis by the teacher, 3) a letter oriented lesson based on the student's error pattern, 4) writing a story the child has composed, 5) reassembling a cut-up story, 6) introducing a new book, 7) and reading a new book. The program contains no standard sequence of materials, though the selection of books is arranged in a sequence of 20 levels.

***Clinical Utility:*** A number of studies have been carried out to determine the effectiveness of *Reading Recovery,* with most indicating favorable results (Center, et. al., 1995). Nevertheless, it should be noted that most studies of *Reading Recovery* were not on low achieving students, and not necessarily learning disabled students. In addition, it should be noted that *Reading Recovery* students performed superior to controls on tests measuring reading achievement, but not on tests measuring metalinguistic types of skills (Center, et. al, 1995). This is because *Reading Recovery,* at best, uses an ***analytical*** phonetic approach as whole words are introduced first, and phonemic awareness skills are taught embedded within these words. Since the emphasis of this approach is certainly not on phonemic awareness skills, caution should be given when using this on dysphonetic or mixed types of dyslexias. The safe bet is that *Reading Recovery* will help in fluency and comprehension, and should be used with low achieving readers or surface dyslexics, both of whom have some level phonetic mastery. From a neuropsychological standpoint, much emphasis is placed on automatic recognition of words, which involves the insular cortex in the neural circuitry of reading.

**LINDAMOOD PHONEMIC SEQUENCING PROGRAM (LIPS):** This program was developed by Charles and Patricia Lindamood, a linguist and speech pathologist, and was formerly known as **Auditory Discrimination in Depth (ADD).** The basis lies on the ability to identify and classify speech sounds, and all sounds have been categorized on the basis of shape and the position of the lips, teeth, and tongue when presented. As students become familiar with the mouth actions that produce speech sounds, this awareness becomes the means of verifying sounds within words, and enables individuals to become self-correcting in both reading and spelling. Thus, the key strategy to reading instruction lies in utilizing another sensory modality: namely, feeling, to provide the brain conscious input with respect to sound classification. The underlying cause of difficulty in responding to literacy instruction presumably is an undeveloped auditory conceptual/phonological awareness. Hence, reading disorders are merely a byproduct of this subtle neurological dysfunction. Students learn to distinguish and name various sound categories using colored blocks to distinguish phonemes. Once students become proficient at encoding sounds, regular and irregular words are introduced, and finally at the last level, reading takes place. The *Lindamood* program is a visual/language based type of instruction focusing on phonological awareness training. It does not include readers, and minimal coverage is given to reading comprehension.

**Clinical Utility:** There is little research on using the *Lindamood* program on students with developmental dyslexia. Research by Lyon (1985) has suggested that any explicit phonics approach may place inordinate demands on the weak phonological system of dyslexic children, and these children might be better served by reading instruction that does not require as much storage, manipulation, and blending of individual phonemes. However, some longitudinal research (Torgeson & Hecht, 1996) has yielded encouraging results using *Lindamood's* training in conjunction with an actual synthetic phonological approach. Once again, using a methodology that specifically targets phonemic awareness will have better success with younger students than with secondary students given the plasticity of the brain to learn these skills at an earlier age (Rourke, 1994). From a neuropsychological standpoint, this system focuses heavily on strengthening the production of sounds: namely Broca's area in the prefrontal cortex, as a primary means to strengthen the neural circuitry of reading in children. Additionally, the program may help strengthen the integrity of the arcuate fasciculus, which helps to map connecting the sounds that children hear (Wernicke's area) with the sounds that children produce (Broca's area).

**DISTAR:** The *Direct Instruction Model* was originally designed for disadvantaged students in the late 1960s, and follows a very regimented script. Students are taught in small

groups and the program is very much a synthetic or direct phonics program. The reading mastery program has six levels, with pre-reading activities starting as young as preschool. Lessons begin by first identifying letter sounds, and games are introduced to promote sequencing sounds. There is a heavy emphasis on rhyming as a way to help children blend initial sounds. Reading begins when six sounds have been learned. Comprehension activities at the pre-reading level include interpreting pictures and ordering events in sequence. The teacher uses hand signals to direct the activities, and an interesting distinction is made between slowly sounding out words vs. pronouncing words in a rapid manner. The recommended time for reading instructions is 30 minutes of group instruction followed by 20 minutes of independent work.

***Clinical Utility:*** One of the most frequent criticisms of the *DISTAR* method from teachers is that scripted lessons place too many restrictions on the instructor. There is virtually no research on the effectiveness of *DISTAR* with dyslexic children. According to Torgeson & Hecht (1996), there is still much debate as to whether traditional synthetic models of phonics instruction are more effective than analytic models of instruction that emphasize teaching phonics within the context of whole word reading. The traditional synthetic models, such as *DISTAR* or the *Orton-Gillingham* approach, are more *"bottom up"* methods of teaching, while the analytic models are more *"top down"* methods of teaching. There should not be a debate between these types of phonetic approaches as both can be highly effective if matched with a student's neurodevelopmental profile. It is recommended that dysphonetic dyslexics might benefit from a more analytic approach to learning phonics, since these readers over-rely on visual cues in a *"top down"* type of manner. However, surface dyslexics might benefit from a more synthetic approach to phonics since these readers use a more auditory, *"bottom-up"* approach to reading. Once again, for dyslexics in secondary school, most of who are beyond the age for the brain to make critical phoneme classifications, neither approach may work. From a neuropsychological standpoint, this system focuses on strengthening the integrity of the phonological loop between the superior temporal gyrus and angular gyrus.

***PROJECT READ:*** *Project Read* is a mainstream language arts program that was initiated in 1981 for students who need direct (explicit) phonics instruction. There are three specific strands to the curriculum that includes: 1) decoding skills, 2) reading comprehension, and 3) written expression. Decoding skills are organized around a traditional sequence of letter sounds with short vowels first, followed by long vowels, vowel digraphs, and then polysyllabic vowels. *Project Read* can be used as an early intervention program for grades one through six, as well as with secondary students and adults. Vocabulary building is an essential framework to the program, and *Project Read*

also focuses on test taking strategies for older students as well. Teacher training for the program involves a three-day summer institute, and daily instruction involves the use of scripts.

***Clinical Utility:*** *Project Read* was not necessarily designed for students with dyslexia, though the intense phonics program provides a highly structured format for younger students with dysphonetic dyslexia. As with any *scripted* program, some teachers may have some reservations and be discouraged by the lack of flexibility. In addition, the comprehension component might be somewhat cumbersome for special education students, as much emphasis is placed on graphing or outlining main characters, setting, and major themes. As with any synthetic or direct phonics program, this system focuses on strengthening the integrity of the phonological loop between the superior temporal gyrus and angular gyrus.

**<u>GREAT LEAPS READING:</u>** The *Great Leaps Reading* program is an individualized reading program designed for students ranging from kindergarten through adulthood. There are three basic components: 1) developing essential phonological awareness, 2) developing sight phrases to build vocabulary awareness, and 3) enhancing reading fluency. Unlike other reading programs, much emphasis is directed toward student motivation and rewarding positive outcomes. The program takes pride in being very simplistic and claims that no more than 10 minutes per day is required to build essential reading skills. The K-2 program offers sound awareness activities to build a solid reading foundation for the emergent reader.

***Clinical Utility:*** One of the benefits of the *Great Leaps* program is the flexibility of the material, which can be used for beginning readers as well as adults. However, its relative simplicity as well as its claims of only 5 to 10 minutes a day leaves one a bit skeptical. Nevertheless, this program was designed for dyslexic readers as well as students with mild cognitive impairments, and can be effective in building fluency skills among older students. The program boasts that 75 percent of the students in the pilot program who were in 6th grade began the reading program reading at a 1st grade level and became independent readers once leaving middle school. Nevertheless, most beginning readers need far more than 5 to 10 minutes a day building phonemic awareness skills. Therefore, this program might be most effective when used as a complement to another reading series. From a neuropsychological standpoint, the *Great Leaps* program focuses on enhancing the neural components involved in building fluency and automatizing the reading process; namely, the insular cortex.

## STRATEGIES FOR OLDER STUDENTS:

Though the primary emphasis has been on developmental dyslexia, there remains exciting new strategies more applicable for older students and adult nonreaders. Notice the primary emphasis among these approaches lies more in the realm of language structure and teaching executive functioning skills as opposed to direct instruction in the decoding or phonemic process. Once again, successful programs have targeted brain developmental areas still undergoing myelination, namely, the frontal lobes, to address skills such as planning, organization, strategy formation, and self-monitoring to assist in the reading process. Some of the more effective strategies and programs include the following:

**_WILSON READING SYSTEM:_** The _Wilson Reading System_ is one of the few remedial programs designed specifically for adults and adolescents with dyslexia. This is a relatively new system, developed within the last decade that is based on many of the _Orton-Gillingham_ principles to teaching reading. There is a heavy emphasis on learning six syllable types, and words are underlined by syllables. Finger tapping is used to analyze spoken words into phonemes for spelling. The actual lesson plans follow seven basic steps: 1) Sound cards (color coded) introduce a new sound, 2) Word cards then practice the newly learned sound, 3) Word list reading, 4) Sentence reading, 5) Preparation for written work, 6) Written work, and 7) Reading and listening.

**_Clinical Utility:_** The _Wilson Reading System_ offers a unique change from the traditional reading programs, many of which are geared toward beginning readers in early elementary school. This program emphasizes the structure of language as opposed to phonics knowledge. In other words, this program emphasizes the metacognitive skills necessary to understand that language is comprised of a series of sounds that occupy a certain temporal order. Much more focus is spent on syllable recognition than on low-level, paired associations between graphemes and morphemes. From a neuropsychological standpoint, much emphasis is based upon strengthening the phonological circuitry from the angular gyrus on to more higher levels of processing. The system was actually designed for language-based learning disabled children, or dysphonetic dyslexics, and represents a promising approach for older students.

**_SRA CORRECTIVE READING:_** The _SRA Corrective Reading_ program allows students to work in a decoding program, a comprehension program, or both. Each program has four levels, and placement tests are provided so that students may enter at the appropriate instructional level. The comprehension program focuses on vocabulary development,

inferential reasoning, and teaching metacognitive strategies to develop higher order thinking and problem solving. The lessons are scripted, though flexible enough to allow students to build on previously acquired skills and abilities. Conversely, the decoding program teaches fluency by teaching letter sounds and blending skills and then applying these strategies to reading expository passages typical of textbook material. Both the decoding and the comprehension programs are designed for students in grades 4 through 12. Teachers need to be trained in the program, and ongoing assessments allow teachers to adjust the learning pace.

**_Clinical Utility:_** The authors claim that a number of studies have evaluated the effectiveness of _SRA Corrective Reading_ for students with learning disabilities and children with lower IQs. Most results have shown encouraging signs, especially with students who have not responded to more conventional reading programs. Once again, this is one of the few reading programs designed for secondary students with learning difficulties. Much of the emphasis lies in developing appropriate executive functioning skills, namely, those cognitive characteristics that allow for the appropriate organization, planning, and monitoring of behavior so that meaningful learning can commence. From a neuropsychological perspective, much emphasis is placed on enhancing frontal lobe functioning because this region plays a key role in reading comprehension. For instance, the ability to pay attention to several components at once, grasp the gist of complex situations, resist distractions, and anticipate future behavior all are mediated by this brain region and vital metacognitive skills for effective reading comprehension. Therefore, _SRA Corrective Reading_ seems to be a good resource for students with deep dyslexia or other reading comprehension difficulties.

**NEUROLOGICAL IMPRESS:** The _Neurological Impress_ method was designed specifically to increase fluency, correct pronunciation and phrasing, and increase confidence in reading. The program is relatively simple as the instructor sits on the handedness side of the student and reads aloud with the student. While tracking the words with a finger, the instructor then begins to read a little faster and a little louder than the student. Occasionally, the instructor will lower the volume of their voice to allow the student to lead in the reading exercise. There are no specific books recommended, though this methodology of reading instruction allows for immediate feedback for the student. Also, there is no emphasis on phonemic awareness skills as fluency and speed are greatly emphasized.

**_Clinical Utility:_** The _Neurological Impress_ method is a very specific type of instructional approach, and not recommended for beginning readers. There is little emphasis on

phonics instruction, vocabulary building, or comprehension activities. The program presupposes the student is capable of reading at some level of independent mastery, and needs to target building fluency and mechanics. This may work best with surface dyslexics, who have great difficulty automatizing the reading process, as each individual phoneme is broken down in a slow, laborious process. From a neuropsychological standpoint, the *Neurological Impress* method was designed specifically toward automatizing the reading process; namely, allowing the insular cortex to take command.

**LAUBACH WAY TO READING:** The *Laubach Way to Reading* and writing series was developed primarily for adults with little or no reading ability. This program may also be used with high school dropouts or students in intermediate grades who need remedial work in basic skills. The series consists of four skill books, which can be administered by a teacher, aide, or tutor. There are also correlated readers for student use. The first skill book begins on a zero level and lays a foundation for decoding by teaching sounds and names of letters. The second skill book structures lessons around short vowel sounds, introduces digraphs, and introduces basic sentence writing. The third skill book presents long sounds and more emphasis is placed on comprehension, recognizing main ideas, and predicting outcomes. In addition, cursive writing is taught at this level. The fourth skill book examines irregular vowel sounds and other consonant spellings. There is more emphasis placed on reading speed and fluency as well as inferential thinking to develop greater comprehension. Each skill book follows a standard format, including sound/symbol charts, short readings, vocabulary, a review of previous lessons, and a writing exercise.

**Clinical Utility:** There are very few reading series for adults who are nonreaders, with the *Laubach* series and *Starting Over* by Joan Knight being just two. Nevertheless, these programs were not necessarily designed for adults with disabilities or adults who lost a previously acquired skill through brain injury, and therefore assume a certain amount of neural integrity within the brain. Unfortunately, many adults who are illiterate have co-existing emotional conditions that greatly hinder any formalized reading instructional program, or have significant neural deficits interfering with learning. Still, the *Laubach* series is a highly comprehensive approach that attempts to retrain the entire neurological circuitry involved with reading in addition to focusing on executive functioning skills to assist with comprehension skills.

## TABLE 11-4

| SUMMARY OF REMEDIATION APPROACHES |
|---|

### PHONOLOGICAL DYSLEXIA

**Remediations:**

**Under Age 7:**
Fast ForWord (Tallal)
Earobics I
Phono-Graphix
Lindamood Phonemic Sequencing Program (LIPS)

**Ages 7 - 12:**
Alphabetic Phonics (Orton-Gillingham)
Slingerland
VAKT approach
Project Read
Lindamood Phonemic Sequencing Program (LIPS)

**Over Age 12:**
Wilson Reading System
SRA Corrective Reading

---

### SURFACE DYSLEXIA

**Remediations:**

**Under Age 7:**
Analytic or Embedded Phonics Approach
DISTAR
Reading Recovery

**Ages 7 -12:**
Great Leaps Reading
Neurological Impress method

**Over Age 12:**
Neurological Impress method
Wilson Reading System
Laubach Reading SerieS

---

### MIXED OR DEEP DYSLEXIA

**Remediations:** An eclectic approach capitalizing on the neurodevelopemental strengths of the child. Use multisensory or any of the aforementioned programs depending upon the age, skill level, and neurodevelopmental profile of the child.

---

## TABLE 11-5

**SUMMARY OF READING DEVELOPMENT AND INSTRUCTIONAL APPROACHES**

(Beitchman & Young, 1997)

| Reading Stage | Skills to Be Learned | Deficits Associated with RD | Instructional Approaches |
|---|---|---|---|
| Prereading (preschool age) | • Recognition of letter names and some words (e.g., own name)<br>• Beginning of phonological awareness (e.g., awareness of similarities/ differences between phonemes, nursery rhyme knowledge) | • Limited knowledge of rhyme, letter names<br>• Slowness in naming highly familiar visual stimuli (e.g., objects, colors, numbers) | Training in phonemic awareness (programs that draw attention to sound patterns in words), training in the alphabet-letter names and corresponding sounds |
| Decoding Stage (beginning grades 1 and 2) | • Use of letter cues to decode words<br>• Basic corres-pondences between letters or letter combinations and sounds | • Limited phonological processing skills<br>• Few words recognized by "sight"<br>• Sounding out of words is often in-accurate, as is spelling | Phonics programs that emphasize letter-sound correspondences, whether in isolation or in the context of words |
| Transitional Reader (beginning in grades 2 and 3) | • Gain fluency<br>• Integrate decoding and context cues<br>• Decode automatically and with less con-scious effort so that resources can be allocated to com-prehension of text | • Reading lacks fluency and expressives, although generally accurate<br>• Reading comprehension is limited | Repeated reading of slightly challenging text to improve fluency and comprehension |
| Fluent, Independent, Functional Reading | • Oral reading is fluent and expressive<br>• Silent reading for comprehension or information makes up the majority of reading activity | • Comprehension problems due to poor comprehension-monitoring, working memory limitations, and limited domain knowledge | Teaching of reading comprehension, metacognitive and memory-enhancing strategies (e.g., self-interrogation, use of rehearsal and elabor-ation), use of advance organizers to access background knowledge and organize information |

# epilogue

Educators have pondered the efficacy of reading instruction for decades in the lofty hopes of eradicating illiteracy among children in our country. Phonics versus whole language approaches have dominated the discourse and set the trend for a wave of remediation strategies, each claiming to be better than the next. Fueled by politics, money, or the self-centered grandeur of solving the cognitive riddle of literacy, many well-crafted educational approaches have fallen short of expectations. Yet the methods of science have taught us that prior to finding a solution to a problem, it behooves us to formulate the right hypothesis and ask the right question. Until recently, most assumed that reading disabilities stemmed from inadequate reading instruction; consequently, the biological underpinnings of literacy had often been ignored. This placed the emphasis on finding a *magic bullet* type of remediation approach. As we head into the 21st century, a new question has been formulated in the educational remediation of dyslexia. Drawing upon the technological advances from the neurosciences, the testing creativity of neuropsychology, and the innovative strategies of the educational community, we can now reformulate the question as being: *"What is the functional integrity of the neural pathways which modulate reading in a given child's brain?"* A working knowledge of brain/behavior relationships remains essential for psychologists to accurately diagnose reading disorders, as well as for professional educators to build literacy skills. Embracing the richness of these disciplines while working within a scientific framework should lead to the educational remediation of dyslexia, as well as shed insight on another layer of knowledge of our species. After all, there is no one body of knowledge with all the answers to human cognitive functioning, though history has shown us one pathway worth taking the journey: science.

# APPENDIX I

## TEACHER CHECKLIST FOR DYSLEXIC BEHAVIORS

Make a check mark by each statement that is indicative of the student's behavior. If you have checked a total of six or more statements, the student may be dyslexic.

### Characteristic Behaviors of Dysphonetic Dyslexia

The student ...
- [ ] 1. maintains a strong performance for leisure and academic activities that involve minimal listening skills.
- [ ] 2. can comprehend more efficiently when material is read silently rather than orally.
- [ ] 3. prefers learning from silent media (films) rather than audio media (tapes).
- [ ] 4. has difficulty recalling everyday words in conversation.
- [ ] 5. takes wild guesses recalling everyday words in conversation.
- [ ] 6. has extreme difficulty blending letter sounds.
- [ ] 7. remembers better when shown what to do than told what to do.
- [ ] 8. experiences difficulty in remembering information (e.g., class assignments, phone messages) without making written notes.
- [ ] 9. makes many spoonerisms ("You hissed classed today" for "you missed class today").
- [ ] 10. does not follow oral directions well.
- [ ] 11. omits vowels in two syllable words such as when spelling "tkn" for "taken".
- [ ] 12. substitutes vowels, such as spelling the word "bit" for "bed".

## Characteristic Behaviors of Surface Dyslexia

The student ...
- [ ] 1. consistently uses finger or pencil to maintain place during reading.
- [ ] 2. has difficulty copying information (from chalkboard or paper).
- [ ] 3. mixes up capital and small letters when writing (e.g., dAd)
- [ ] 4. often fails to notice changes in the environment.
- [ ] 5. has difficulty reading maps.
- [ ] 6. has difficult time remembering directions when walking.
- [ ] 7. spells better aloud than in writing. Often gives the correct letters, but in wrong sequence (e.g., "hte" for "the").
- [ ] 8. has difficulty describing visual characteristics of familiar people and places.
- [ ] 9. prefers listening to audio tapes rather than watching films.
- [ ] 10. experiences difficulty when copying figures and signs in mathematics.
- [ ] 11. omits words (and lines of words) when reading.
- [ ] 12. excessive vocalization during silent reading.
- [ ] 13. has a better memory for what is said than for what was read.

## Characteristic Behaviors of Mixed Dyslexia

The student ...
- [ ] 1. has difficulty structuring time.
- [ ] 2. is rigid and inflexible.
- [ ] 3. makes frequent negative comments regarding reading tasks.
- [ ] 4. has a low frustration tolerance (especially during reading activities).
- [ ] 5. is highly distractible.
- [ ] 6. seems unaware of nonverbal social cues (e.g., gestures, tone of voice).
- [ ] 7. has difficulty making friends often due to blunt and insensitive remarks.
- [ ] 8. has not benefitted from instruction via typical basal reading programs.

# APPENDIX 11

## INFORMAL PHONOLOGICAL AWARENESS TEST

### *RHYMING*

<u>DISCRIMINATION</u>

Directions: "I'm going to say two words and ask you if they rhyme. Listen carefully."

Demonstration item: "*Fan* rhymes with *man.* Do *rat* and *mat* rhyme?"

Additional demonstration items: *lag/log, mitt/fit*

1. book/look  (yes)
2. un/run    (yes)
3. ring/rat  (no)
4. box/yes   (no)
5. fish/dish  (yes)

<u>PRODUCTION</u>

Directions: "I'm going to say a word and I want you to tell me a word that rhymes with it. Listen carefully." (Note. Nonsense words are acceptable.)

Demonstration item: "Tell me a word that rhymes with *bat.*"

Additional demontration items: *miss, log*

1. cat
2. pot
3. tame
4. wrinkle
5. brother

## *SEGMENTING COMPOUND WORDS*

Directions: "I'm going to say some big words made up of two little words. I want you to clap one time for each little word. Listen carefully."

Demonstration item: *"mousetrap"* (model clapping)

Additional demonstration items: *birdhouse, football*

1. cupcake
2. mailbox
3. horseshoe
4. snowman
5. bedtime

## *SEGMENTING SYLLABLES*

Directions: "I'm going to say a word and I want yu to clap one time for eeach beat or syllable. Listen carefully."

Demonstration item: *"bicycle"* (model clapping)

Additional demonstration items: *cat, summer*

1. house
2. garden
3. pocket
4. fantastic
5. dinosaur

## *ISOLATING PHONEMES*

<u>INITIAL POSITION</u>

Directions: "I'm going to say a word and ask you to tell me the beginning or first sound of the word. Listen carefully."

Demonstration item: Say *"cat."* Then ask, "What's the beginning sound of *cat?*"

Additional demonstration items: dog, mouse

| | | | |
|---|---|---|---|
| 1. bite | (b) | 4. dinosaur | (d) |
| 2. toy | (t) | 5. fudge | (f) |
| 3. purple | (p) | | |

## *FINAL POSITION*

Directions: "I'm going to say a word and ask you to tell me the ending or last sound of the word. Listen carefully."

Demonstration item: Say *"cat."* Then ask, "What's the ending sound of *cat?*"

Additional demonstration items: *duck, fish*

| | | | |
|---|---|---|---|
| 1. bug | (g) | 4. bush | (sh) |
| 2. house | (s) | 5. math | (th) |
| 3. rat | (t) | | |

## *BLENDING PHONEMES*

Directions: "I'll say the sounds of a word. You guess what word it is. Listen carefully."

Demonstration item: Say these sounds with a very short pause between them *"/i/.../t/."* What word did I say?

Additional demonstration items: */u/.../p/* (up), */p/.../o/.../p/* (pop)

Say each word slowly by phoneme as indicated.

1. b - oy        (boy)
2. s - i - t      (sit)
3. t - ai - l     (tail)
4. f - l - a - g   (flag)
5. k - i - n - d  (kind)

## *SEGMENTING PHONEMES*

Directions: "I'm going to say a word and I want you to say each sound in the word. Listen carefully."

Demonstration item: Say *"cat."* Then say the individual sounds, pausing slightly between each one. *"/k/.../a/.../t/"*

Additional demonstration items: *up, pig*

1. at          (a - t)
2. game        (g - a - m)
3. keep        (k - e - p)
4. mist        (m - i - s - t)
5. smoke       (s - m - o - k)

- - - - - - - - - - - - - - - - - - - - - - - - - - - - - - - - - - - - -

### SCORING KEY
0-1 Not Mastered
2-3 Not Mastered/Emergent
4-5 Mastered

# APPENDIX III

## MULTISENSORY APPROACHES TO LANGUAGE INSTRUCTION

The instructional programs described below employ a structured, multisensory approach to reading and writing. While this list does not begin to include all available programs that use this methodology, it can serve as a beginning for matching students and programs. Unless stated otherwise, programs are based on the original works of Anna Gillingham and Dr. Samuel Orton.* Studies verifying the success rates of all programs are available. With the exception of Great Leaps and Morphographs, all programs have accompanying training components.

**Alphabetic Phonics** (Texas Scottish Rite Hospital for Children, Dyslexia Therapy)
2222 Welborn Street
Dallas, TX 75219-3993        (214) 559-7425
This is the program Frederick County has adopted. It was developed primarily by Aylett R. Cox and is a sequential, multisensory curriculum for teaching the language skills of reading, writing, spelling and talking, emphasizing phonics, linguistics, and the structure and science of the English language.

**Concept Phonics**
Oxton House Publishers
Farmington, ME 04938        1-800-539-READ
This program is centered on four features, concept training, automaticity, memory strategies, and flexibility. It is a multisensory, structured, phonics-based program that emphasizes fluency, adjustment to learning needs of individual students, and ways to help students retain and use what they learn.

---

*Dr. Samuel T. Orton (1879-1948), a professor of neuro-psychiatry and neuro-pathology at Columbia University was a pioneer in focusing attention on language differences by bringing together neuropsychiatric information and principles of remediation. As early as 1925, he had identified the syndrome of developmental reading disability, separated it from mental defect and brain damage and offered a physiological explanation with a favorable prognosis. Working with Dr. Orton, a teacher, Anna Gillingham (1878-1964), further developed procedures in an organized presentation. Their manual, published in 1935, is now in its seventh edition.

## Great Leaps

Diarmuid, Inc.
Post Office Box 138
Micanopy, FL                    (352) 466-3878
This curriculum is designed as a supplementary reading tutorial program for students ages six through adult. Reading automaticity is learned through repeated practice with oral readings in phonics, sight words embedded in phrases, and one-page short stories.

## The Herman Method

4700 Tyrone Ave.
Sherman Oaks, CA 91423          (818) 784-9566
The *Herman Method for Reversing Reading Failure* is a multisensory, phonetic approach designed for dyslexic students ages eight through adult. It uses kinesthetic and tactile input while teaching a phonetic, structured, sequential reading curriculum. Unique features include deliberate, simultaneous input to both cerebral hemispheres, metronomic pacing to encourage fluency, and multimedia materials.

## Lindamood-Bell Learning Processes

416 Higuera St.
San Luis Obispo, CA 93401       (805) 541-3836
This tri-faceted program incorporates the concept of intensive treatment, a familiar concept in the medical world which has been found to be extremely effective in the learning world. Lindamood's *Visualizing and Verbalizing* program addresses language comprehension and thinking problems resulting from the inability to create an imaged gestalt. The *Drawing with Language Program* develops the uses of language to guide visual-motor problem solving. Word attack, word recognition, and spelling problems are addressed in a third program that incorporates a strong phonological awareness component focusing on the motor-kinesthetic features of speech sounds.

## Morphographs

Science Research Associates
A corrective spelling program that introduces common spelling patterns through morphology. Students learn to read, spell, and understand the meanings of base and root words to which prefixes and suffixes have been added. Rules and patterns of the language are emphasized in the course.

## Phono-Graphix

Read America                    1-800-READ-TO-U

This program that provides a linguistic-phonetic approach to teaching reading with training in phoneme awareness, phoneme-to-grapheme correspondences, and controlled vocabularies. *Phono-Graphix* is designed primarily for younger students who are learning to read and older, remedial reading students.

## Project Read/Language Circle

PO Box 20631
Bloomington, MN 55420      (612) 884-4880

A mainstream language arts program that provides an alternative to whole word, inductive instruction, *Project Read* is designed for the child/adolescent who needs a systematic, direct, multisensory learning experience. Designed to be delivered in the regular classroom, the program has also been successfully implemented in Chapter 1 and special education settings. Designed as an early intervention program for grades 1-6, it can be used with adolescents and adults as well. The program is comprised of several strands including reading, writing, and spelling.

## RAVE-O Program

(Retrieval, Automaticity, Vocabulary or Elaboration, and Othography)
M. Wolf and L. Miller, 1997

A comprehensive, fluency-based intervention that is a direct outgrowth of the double-deficit hypothesis. It directly addresses the need for automaticity in phonological, orthographic, and semantic systems. It works to increase processing speed and improve reading outcomes. A central emphasis is the quick recognition of the most frequent orthographic letter patterns in English. This program is not commercially available. It is, however, described in the *Annals of Dyslexia,* 1999, pp. 3-28.

## The Slingerland Institute

One Bellevue Center
411 108th Ave. NE. 230
Bellevue, WA 98004          (206) 453-1190

The Slingerland Approach is a simultaneous, multisensory approach that begins with a single unit of sight, sound, or thought, and proceeds to the more complex. Emphasis is on teaching through intellect and building understanding of concepts rather than rote learning. The daily program integrates 3 modalities of language learning in a structured, sequential approach. The goal is for the student to compose propositional and creative writing. The Visual Approach leads to independent reading of the student's choice.

**The Spalding Education Foundation**

15410 N. 67th Ave., Suite 8

Glendale, AZ 85306          (602) 486-5881

A total language arts method that integrates listening and reading comprehension, speaking, and writing. It is designed to challenge students who have facility with language as well as those who have great difficulty learning. The program is designed primarily for beginning readers or older students at that level.

**Wilson Language Training**

162 West Main St.

Millbury, MA 01527          (508) 865-5699

This program directly teaches the structure of words in the English language so that students master the phonological coding system for reading and spelling. The material is presented in 12 steps in a systematic, sequential and cumulative manner. Teaching techniques utilize visual-auditory-kinesthetic-tactile methods. Materials include phonetically controlled readers that are geared for older students.

# REFERENCES

Amen, D.G. (1997). *Images into the Mind.* Fairfield, CA: MindWorks Press.

Badian, N.A., McAnulty, G.B., & Duffy, F.H. (1990). Prediction of dyslexia in kindergarten boys. *Annals of Dyslexia,* 40, 152-169.

Bakker, D.J. (1992). Neuropsychological classification and treatment of dyslexia. *Journal of Learning Disabilities,* 25, 102-109.

Bateman, B. (1979). Teaching reading to learning disabled and other hard to teach children. In *Theory and Practice of Early Reading,* Vol 1, eds. L.B. Resnick and P.A. Weaver. Hillside, NJ: Lawrence Erlbaum Associates.

Beaton, A.A. (1997). The relation of planum temporale asymmetry and morphology of the corpus callosum to handedness, gender, and dyslexia: A review of the evidence. *Brain and Language,* 60, 225-322.

Beitchman, J.H. & Young, A.R. (1997). Learning disorders: With a special emphasis on reading disorders: A review of the past 10 years. *Journal of the American Academy of Child and Adolescent Psychiatry,* 36 (8), 1020-1030.

Calvin, W.H. & Ojeman, G.A. (1994). *Conversations with Neil's Brain: The Neural Nature of Thought and Language.* Reading, MA: Addison-Wesley Publishing Company.

Carter, R. (1998). *Mapping the Mind.* Berkeley: University of California Press.

Center, Y., Wheldall, K., Freeman, L., Outhred, L., & McNaught, M. (1995). An evaluation of reading recovery. *Reading Research Quarterly,* 30 (2), 240-263.

Chase, C.H. (1996). Neurobiology of learning disabilities. *Seminars in Speech and Language,* 17 (3), 173-181.

Clark, D.B. & Uhry, J.K. (1995). *Dyslexia: Theory and Practice of Remedial Instruction.* Baltimore: York Press, Inc.

Demb, J.B., Boynton, G.M., & Heeger, D.J. (1998). Brain activity in visual cortex predicts individual differences in reading performance. *Proceedings from the National Academy of Science,* 94, 13363.

Denckla, M.B. & Rudel, R.G. (1976). Naming of object drawings by dyslexic and other learning disabled children. *Brain & Language,* 3, 1-15.

DeFries, J.C., Olsen, R.K., Pennington, B.F., & Smith, S.D. (1991). Colorado reading project: An update. *In The Reading Brain: The Biological Basis of Dyslexia,* eds. D. Duane and D. Gray. Parkton, MD: York Press.

Duara, R., Kushch, A., & Gross-Glenn, K. (1991). Neuroanatomical differences between dyslexic and normal readers on magnetic resonance imaging scans. *Archives of Neurology,* 48, 410-416.

Filley, C.M. (1995). *Neurobehavioral Anatomy.* Niwot, CO: University Press of Colorado.

Flowers, L. (1993). Brain basis for dyslexia: A summary of work in progress. *Journal of Learning Disabilities,* 26, 575-582.

Galaburda, A.M., Rosen, G.D., & Sherman, G.F. (1990). Individual variability in cortical organization: Relationship to brain laterality and implications to function. *Neuropsychologia,* 28, 529-546.

Geschwind, N. & Galaburda, A.M. (1985). Cerebral lateralization: Biological mechanisms, associations, and pathology: III. A hypothesis and a program for research. *Archives of Neurology,* 42, 634-654.

Goldberg, E. (1989). Gradiental approach to neocortical functional organization. *Journal of Clinical and Experimental Neuropsychology,* 11, 4, 489-517.

Goldberg, E. & Costa, L. (1981). Hemispheric differences in the acquisition and use of descriptive systems. *Brain and Language,* 14, 144-173.

Hart, B. & Risley, T. (1995). *Meaningful differences.* Baltimore: Brookes.

Horwitz, B., Rumsey, J.M., & Donohue, B.C. (1998). Functional connectivity of the angular gyrus in normal reading and dyslexia. *Proceedings of the National Academy of Science, USA,* 95, 8939-8944.

Hutcheson, L., Selig, H., & Young, N. (1990). A success story: A large urban district offers a working model for implementing multisensory teaching into the resource and regular classroom. *Annals of Dyslexia,* 40, 79-96.

Hurford, D.P., Schauf, J.D., Bunce, L., Blaich, T., & Moore, K. (1994). Early identification of children at risk for reading disabilities. *Journal of Learning Disabilities,* 27 (6), 371-382.

Hynd, C. (1986). Educational intervention in children with developmental learning disorders. *Child Neuropsychology,* 2, 265-297.

Hynd, G.W. & Cohen, M. (1983). *Dyslexia: Neuropsychological theory, research, and clinical differentiation.* Orlando: Hartcourt Brace Jovanovich, Publishers.

Hynd, G.W., Hall, J., Novey, E.S., Eliopulos, R.T., Black, K., Gonzalez, J.J., Edmonds, J.E., Riccio, C., & Cohen, M. (1995). Dyslexia and corpus callosum morphology. *Archives of Neurology,* 52, 32-38.

Hynd, G.W., Marshall, R.M., & Clikeman, M.S. (1991). Developmental dyslexia, neurolinguistic theory, and deviations in brain morphology. *Reading and writing: An Interdisciplinary Journal,* 3, 345-362.

Hynd, G.W. & Semund-Clikeman, M. (1989). Dyslexia and brain morphology. *Psychological Bulletin,* 106, 447-482.

Jarvis, P.E. & Barth, J.T. (1994). The Halstead-Reitan *Neuropsychological Battery: A guide to interpretation and clinical applications.* Odessa, FL: Psychological Assessment Resources.

Kaufman, A.S. (1994). *Intelligent Testing with the WISC III.* New York: John Wiley & Sons, Inc.

Kotulak, R. (1997). *Inside the Brain.* Kansas City: Andrews McMeel Publishing.

Kolb, B. & Whishaw, I.Q. (1996). *Fundamentals of human neuropsychology: fourth edition.* New York: W.H. Freeman and Company.

Lovegrove, W. (1993). *Annals of the New York Academy of Science,* 14, 57-59.

Livingstone, M.S., Rosen, G.D., Drislane, F.W., and Galaburda, A.M. (1991). *Proceedings of the National Academy of Science, USA,* 88, 7943-7947.

Lyon, G.R. (1996). Learning Disabilities. *The Future of Children: Special Education for Students with Learning Disabilities,* Vol. 6 (1), 54-73.

Lyon, G.R. (1985). Educational validation studies. In B.P. Rourke (Ed.), *Neuropsychology of Learning Disabilities* (p. 228-253). New York: Guilford.

MacLean, P. (1973). *A Triune Concept of Brain and Behavior.* Toronto, Can.: University of Toronto Press.

Mather, N. (1992). Whole language reading instruction for students with learning disabilities: Caught in the cross fire. *Learning Disabilities Research and Practice,* 7, 87-95.

Matthews, C. (1991). Serial processing and the phonetic route: Lessons learned in the functional reorganization of deep dyslexia. *Journal of Communication Disorders,* 24, 21-39.

McCarthy, R.A. & Warrington, E.K. (1990). *Cognitive Neuropsychology: A clinical introduction.* New York: Academic Press, Inc.

McGuinness, D. (1997). *Why our children can't read and what we can do about it.* New York: Simon & Schuster.

Omstein, R. (1993). *The Roots of the Self: Unraveling the Mystery of Who We Are.* New York: HarperCollins, Publishers.

Paulesu, E., Frith, U., Smowling, M., Gallagher, A., Morton, J., Frackowiak, R.S.J., & Frith, C. (1996). Is developmental dyslexia a disconnection syndrome?, *Brain,* 119, 143-157.

Posner, M.I. & Raichle, M.E. (1994). *Images of the Mind.* New York: W.H. Freeman Company.

Ramachandran, V.S. & Blakeslee, S. (1998). *Phantoms in the Brain.* New York: William Morrow and Company, Inc.

Reitan, R.M. & Wilson, D. (1992). *Neuropsychological evaluation of older children.* South Tuscon Arizona: Neuropsychology Press.

Ridder, W.H., Borting, E., Cooper, M., McNeel, B., & Huang, E. (1997). Not all dyslexics are created equal. *Optometry and Vision Science,* 74, 99-104.

Rosselli, M. (1993). Neuropsychology of illiteracy. *Behavioural Neurology,* 6, 107-112.

Rouke, B.P. & Del Dotto, J. (1994). *Learning Disabilities: A neuropsychological perspective.* New York: Sage Publications.

Sagan, C. (1980). *Cosmos.* New York: Ballantine Books.

Sagan, C. (1996). *The Demon-Haunted World.* New York: Ballantine Books.

Sattler, J.S. (1988). *Assessment of Children.* San Diego: Jerome Sattler Publisher.

Schultze, R.T., Cho, N.K., Staub, L.H., Kier, L.E., Fletcher, J.M., Shaywitz, S.E., Shankweler, D.P., Katz, L., Gore, J.C., Duncan, J.S., & Shaywitz, B.A. (1994). Brain morphology in normal and dyslexic children: The influence of sex and age. *Annal of Neurology,* 35, 732-742.

Shaywitz, S. (1996). Dyslexia, *Scientific American,* 2-8.

Shaywitz, S. (1998). Dyslexia, *The New England Journal of Medicine,* Vol 338, (5), 307-311.

Shaywitz, S.E., Shaywitz, B.A., Pugh, K.R., Fulbright, R.K., Constable, R.T., Mencl, W.E., Shankweiler, D.P., Liberman, A.M., Skudlarski, P., Fletcher, J.M., Katz, L., Marchione, K.E., Lacadie, C., Gatenby, C., & Gore, J.C. (1998). Functional disruption in the organization of the brain for reading in dyslexia. *Proceedings of the National Academy of Science, USA,* 95, 2636-2641.

Siegal, L.S. (1992). An evaluation of the discrepancy definition of dyslexia. *Journal of Learning Disabilities,* 25 (10), 618-629.

Siegal, L.S. (1989). IQ is irrelevant for the definition of learning disabilities. *Journal of Learning Disabilities,* 22 (8), 469-478.

Storfer, M.D. (1990). *Intelligence and Giftedness: The Contributions of Heredity and Early Environment.* San Francisco, CA: Jossey-Bass.

Tallal, P., Miller, S., & Fitch, R.H. (1993). Neurobiological basis of speech. A case for the preeminence of temporal speech. *Annal of the New York Academy of Science,* 682, 27-47.

Torgeson, J. & Hecht, S. (1996). Preventing and remediating reading disabilities: Instructional variables that make a difference for special students. In M.F. Graves, P. Van Den Broek & B.M. Taylor (eds.) *The First R: Every Child's Right To Read* (p. 133-159), Teachers College Press, Newark: DE.

Victor, J.D. (1993). *Visual Neuroscience,* 10, 939-946.

Wolf, M. (1999). What time may tell: Towards a new conceptualization of developmental Dyslexia. *Annal of Dyslexia,* 49, 3-23.

# ABOUT THE AUTHORS

**Philip A. De Fina, Ph.D., ABPdN.,** has extensive training as both a clinical neuropsychologist and school psychologist. He is currently employed as a school psychologist in Howard County, Maryland and is the Director of Graduate/Post-Graduate Neuropsychology Training at the Fielding Institute. Dr. De Fina has an appointment as a Guest Researcher in the Laboratory of Clinical and Experimental Neuropsychology at the National Institute of Mental Health. He is also a member of the international neuroscience subcommittee of the World Health Organization, and is currently president of the American Board of School Neuropsychology. Dr. De Fina is board certified in pediatric clinical neuropsychology.

**Steven G. Feifer, Ed.S., NCSP** is currently employed as a nationally certified school psychologist for Frederick County Public Schools in Frederick, Maryland. He is also a neuropsychological consultant for The Attention and Learning Center of Greater Washington in Silver Spring, MD. Mr. Feifer holds an advanced post-graduate certification in clinical neuropsychology, and has conducted numerous workshops and published various articles on using neuropsychological instruments to assess and remediate learning disorders in children. Specific comments or requests for speaking engagements should be addressed to Feifer@Frederickmd.com.